Doll Collectors Manual 1983

Limited Edition
The Doll Collectors
Of America, Inc.

Printed in the United States of America
Published by HOBBY HOUSE PRESS

Foreward

The committee is pleased to present this Manual, the ninth edition by the Doll Collectors of America, Inc. In keeping with the purpose of the club, the material is offered with the hope of stimulating and encouraging the study, collection and preservation of early dolls.

Acknowledgement

The Manual Committee thanks sincerely the members of the Doll Collectors of America, Inc. who have so generously contributed to the production of this book.

Publication Committee

President Emeritus D.C.A., Inc.	Mrs. Leonard B. Cripps
Chairman	Mrs. Russell T. Burton
Editor	Mrs. Alfred L. Popp
Treasurer	Mrs. Thomas J. Kiley
Business Manager	Mrs. F. J. Donoghue
Advertising Manager	Mrs. Donald J. Marion
Review Committee	Miss Evelyn Jane Coleman
	Mrs. Jon J. Johnston
	Mrs. Richard Merrill
	Miss Ruth E. Whittier

ISBN 087588-194-7

AMELIA POLLARD BOTTOMLEY

The Doll Collectors of America, Inc.
dedicate this 1983 Manual
to
Amelia Pollard Bottomley   Honorary Director
Vice President   1939-1962
President   1962-1965
Her years of devoted service to the Doll Collectors of America, Inc. have had a stimulating
influence on the membership in the pursuit of the club's objectives.

Table of Contents

Mabel Lee - A China Doll of 1854

by Madeline O. Merrill
Photography by Richard Merrill

In November of 1854, Mrs. Priscilla Langdon (Harris) Hooper of Boston, Massachusetts, bought and dressed for her little niece, Fanny Hooper, a 22" pink-toned china headed doll which was named, at the time, "Mabel Lee." The doll and wardrobe, a birthday gift, was passed down through three successive generations of the family with little change other than the doll being renamed "Fanny" in honor of the first recipient.

The child, Fanny, must have been much loved by her aunt, for accompanying the doll and wardrobe, and still preserved, is the following poignant note.

Boston Nov. 27, 1854

My dear little Fanny

The bearer of this note, Mabel Lee, is an orphan, whom your cousins, the Hoopers, found one day. She was very naked, though not very poor, as her plumpness will show. So they concluded to bring her to our house and make her a suit of clothes. After doing this, they could think of no home so agreeable to the young girl as your own dear Mother's house in Greenwood Avenue. She is not to take the place of the other little girl there, but to help her to pass her time agreeably. Perhaps when it is cloudy and cold, she will make sunshine for a little while. If she fails to do this, I advise if she is naughty or cross at all, that you put her into some dark corner or drawer till she is herself again.

May your birthdays all be happy ones, my dear!

From your loving Aunt
(Signed) P. L. Hooper

The doll is now in the Merrill collection and is much prized, as it is not too often we are fortunate enough to have an acquisition of this age with such irrefutable and touching documentation.

Illustration 1. The doll, "Mabel Lee," later called "Fanny." 22" in height. Pink-toned china head has blue painted eyes and rosy cheeks. Centerparted, black painted hair has twelve molded, vertical curls encircling head. Wears dress of brown printed cotton. Underwear, of white cotton, consists of shift, petticoat and pantalettes. The latter two with rows of hemstitched tucks. Stockings are faded red in color and square toed shoes a soft blue-green. Still worn are hand knit mitts which are too fragile to remove. And around her neck still hangs a childishly made necklace of pink ribbon hung with little trifles.

Illustration 2. Original outfit made, in 1854, for china headed doll, "Mabel Lee." *Top* (from left to right): (1) white cotton nightcap with drawstring ties; (2) straw hat with crossed ribbon trim; (3) wool cape trimmed with pleated ribbon bands and lace; (4) small checked silk apron; (5) cotton print dress with puffed sleeves, gathered bodice and skirt cartridge-pleated into waistband, deep hem with tuck in skirt. *Bottom* (from left to right): (6) cotton nightgown with gathered yoke and sleeves, ruffles at neck and cuffs, front-buttoning; (7) lightweight wool, polka dotted dress with piped waistband, yoke, and sleeves of short double ruffles; (8) white cross-barred cotton cape with tasselled hood in modified burnoose style often seen in the mid-nineteenth century.

Hair Styles of Distinction

Collection of Lucie Cripps

Photography by Richard Merrill

Often the hair style of a small china is far more important, to the collector, than the face. For more often than not, the facial structure is quite ordinary. Once in a while a finer detailed face is seen, as in *Illustration 2.*

Illustration 1. Although the face is not visible, it is as interesting as the hair style.

Illustration 2. Shows a fine face of good detail with a popular yet rather plain hair style.

Illustrations 3 and 4. Both have lovely hair styles, yet have ordinary facial modeling and painting.

Illustration 1. 9" pink tint china head, blue eyes, cloth body and limbs.

Illustration 2. 10½" pink tint china head, blue eyes, pink tint arms, cloth legs.

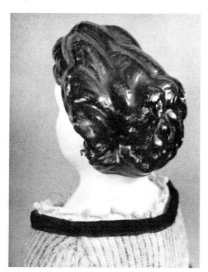

Illustration 3. 9½" white china head and limbs with gold band across front pompadour hair-do, pierced ears, cloth body.

Illustration 4. 9" white china head and limbs, cloth body.

Buying Dolls in Boston

by Evelyn Jane and Dorothy Coleman

Stories abound about the sea captains of the Boston area bringing home dolls for their children. Most dolls over a century ago were imported and a seaport was certainly the most likely place to find them. Dolls were small and would undoubtedly have been a sensible supplement to the cargo of a clipper ship. The various dolls at the Essex Institute and other museums in the Boston environs show us some of the dolls that must have come on these early ships.

But our present interest is in the buying of dolls in Boston once they had arrived. Doll collectors often wish they could go back in time and visit the fascinating toy shops of a century or more ago. Since there is no magic time clock we can at least travel back in our imagination by examining the records of the past.

Buying dolls was a luxury for our ancestors and only the well-to-do could afford to do so. In the 19th century Boston was one of our most affluent cities. The China trade had brought wealth and with it the desire and ability to buy imported baubles which would have included dolls.

Around the middle of the 18th century, William Price had a toy shop next to the "old brick Meeting House in Boston." In 1754 he advertised "London babies, English and Dutch Toys." Of course we know that in the eighteenth century dolls were called "babies" and that the peg-wooden dolls made in the Grödner Tal were called "Dutch" dolls. History tells us that in the late 18th and early 19th centuries salesmen from the Grödner Tal brought their peg-wooden dolls to sell in America. 1754 would probably have been too early for the peg-wooden dolls but no doubt the "Dutch" toys could be interpreted as German toys, which would have included wooden dolls of the types shown in German museums dating from this period.

In the *Boston Annual Advertiser,* 1840 (A Boston Commercial Directory), S. Powell & Co., 36 Cornhill Street was listed as a "London Importing Warehouse . . . Have constantly for sale, at the very lowest rates, the following, viz: . . . LONDON DOLLS AND TOYS, A very large assortment of almost every kind usually kept in large wholesale establishments."

At Winterthur there is a catalog dated 1856 of George N. Davis of Boston who sold rubber heads and rubber dolls. These came painted and unpainted, in white versions and in black versions. Some of the dolls were laughing and some serious. Full length rubber baby dolls were available in these various versions. Other choices of dolls included a Flower Girl, a Soldier, Red Riding Hood, Santa Claus and a doll representing the Daughter of the Regiment.

Another store selling rubber toys and nursery items which probably included dolls was A. S. Jordan at 191 Washington Street where he was located from 1852-67.

As time progressed there were many toy shops in the thriving city of Boston and we can visit only a few of them. The early Directories listed toy shops under Fancy Goods. In 1847 there were 16 stores listed under Fancy Goods on Washington Street and then in 1849 there were only 11. By 1852 there were 19 and by 1867 there were 32 fancy goods establishments on Washington Street. Before 1851 the fancy goods stores were concentrated in the first five blocks of Washington Street. By 1855 they reached to the ninth block, then by 1860 they reached to the eleventh block and in 1867 to the twelfth block.

In 1835 Isaac Cary had been associated with H. Boynton and Philip R. Woodford in the fancy goods line including jewelry and comb making at 54 Washington Street. By 1838 they were at 50 Washington Street. In 1847 Boynton and Philip R. Woodford were operating a fancy goods store at 50 Washington Street where they were also importers and wholesalers.

Orin F. Woodford first appears in the Boston Commercial Directories in 1838 as a clerk working at 50 Washington Street, the place of business of Isaac Cary and Philip Woodford. In 1840 Isaac Cary no longer advertised fancy goods but only the comb making and jewelry. Orin F. Woodford was listed under Fancy Goods with a store at 309 Washington Street, the same address found on several dolls' labels. He continued there until 1855. Only in one 1851 Directory is Woodford & Merrill listed at this address. There are several Merrills listed in other years at other addresses including Geor. Merrill who operated a fancy goods store at 322 Washington Street in 1852. In 1856 Woodford's name disappears from the Directory and Abner Littlefield is found at his address, 309 Washing-

Illustration 1. Boy doll with a black paper label stating that the doll came from the Woodford Fancy Goods Store. China head with a pink tint, blue painted eyes and brown hair with brush marks. Cloth body with wooden arms. Circa 1840-55. Height 13 inches (33 cm.). *Coleman Collection.*

Illustration 2. Close-up of the china head on a doll with the Woodford label. Height of the shoulder head 3¼ inches (8.5 cm.). *Coleman Collection.*

Illustration 3. Label found on the Woodford doll.

Illustration 4. Doll with a Königliche Porzellan Manufakur. (K.P.M.) marked shoulder head on a cloth body labeled "Woodford and Merrill's," kid arms. Circa 1851. Height 19 inches (48 cm.). *Courtesy of the Essex Institute. Photograph by Richard Merrill.*

ton Street, running a fancy goods store. The next year, 1857, J. Wentworth ran a fancy goods store at this same 309 address.

Around the middle of the 19th century (1840-55) some very fine dolls could be purchased at Orin Woodford's shop on Washington Street. Probably Woodford imported the china heads (it is known that Philip Woodford was an importer at one time) and perhaps made the bodies and/or clothes. Two extant china head dolls with similar cloth bodies, except for the arms, bear Woodford labels. Both of these dolls appear to be in original clothes, one of them is dressed in short pants, probably representing a boy while the other wears long pants representing a man. The boy's head is pink china with short brown hair and his arms are wooden. On his chest is a paper label with a shiny black background and gold letters reading, "From WOODFORD'S FANCY STORE, 309 Washington Street, BOSTON." The doll representing a man has a K. P. M. china head marked with the red orb and blue eagle. This doll has kid arms. His label reads, "FROM WOODFORD & MERRILL'S FANCY STORE, 309 Washington Street, BOSTON." (It is listed only in an 1851 Directory as shown above.) Each letter in the word Merrill has a slash through it indicating that the store may have returned to be Woodford only.

In the Warshaw collection at the Smithsonian there is a trade card for O. F. Woodford, 309 Washington Street, Boston, stating that he sells "Toys and Fancy Goods."

Nearby at 336 Washington Street, Nathan Neat had a leather goods store. A dome trunk containing the wardrobe of a fashion-type doll has this name and address on its label. This doll is owned by Madeline Merrill who obtained it from the family of its original owner. For fashion-type dolls let us go to Richard Schwarz's "Toy Emporium" at 497 and 499 Washington Street. The early Directories generally included toys in the fancy goods category but by 1875 toys were listed separately.

In 1875 and 1876 on Washington Street the following stores were listed:

Heyer Brothers, 302 Washington Street (First listed under Fancy Goods in 1855)

Novelty Toy and Basket Store, Horace C. Creech, 462 Washington Street

Dana Dudley, 884 Washington Street

Richard Schwarz at 497 and 499 Washington Street, beginning in 1876.

This was probably one of the finest toy shops in Boston in the 1870s.

Richard Schwarz came to Boston in the late 1840s and no doubt competed with Woodford. An 1878 advertisement for Richard Schwarz tempts us with "elegant French Dolls with Trousseaux; beautiful Wax Dolls of mammoth size; the celebrated French Swimming Doll, and the Unbreakable Jointed Doll so much admired at the Paris Exposition." The picture accompanying the advertisement shows fashion-type dolls dressed as ladies, men and girls. Some of the dolls are "undressed," that is they wear a chemise, a ribbon in their hair and boots. The wax dolls are wax-over composition and came in sizes 8 to 30 inches (20.5 to 76 cm.). The French Swimming Doll must be the Ondine. "The Unbreakable Jointed Doll so much admired at the Paris Exposition" was of course Emile Jumeau's "Bébé Incassable" with a bisque head on a fully jointed composition body which was new at that time. These may have been the "Indestructible Baby Dolls" from 8 to 24 inches (20.5 to 61 cm.), offered from $2.50 up, but the small sizes and low price seem to indicate otherwise. The "French Dolls" all seem to have kid bodies and came in sizes 12, 13½, 15, 18, and 20 inches (30.5, 34, 38, and 51 cm.), priced at $2.00 to $5.00 and more. There were all-bisque and all-china dolls. The black dolls were made of china, rubber or

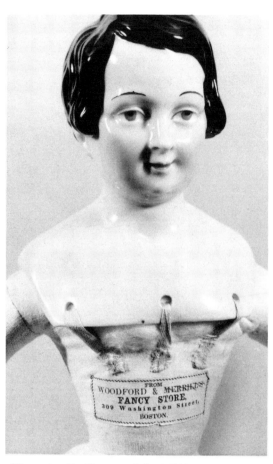

Illustration 5. Close-up of the K.P.M. china head and the "Woodford and Merrill's" label. Height 19 inches (48 cm.). *Courtesy of the Essex Institute. Photograph by Richard Merrill.*

Illustration 6. Close-up of the mark on the K.P.M. doll and the upper portion of the body with the waist seam, a type of construction found on both Woodford dolls. Note that the name "Merrill" is crossed out on this label. *Courtesy of the Essex Institute. Photograph by Richard Merrill.*

12

papier-mâché. Walking and Talking dolls were available. Schwarz also supplied separate heads, bodies, limbs, clothes, accessories and paper patterns for dolls' clothes.

As the 19th century progressed you could buy your dolls in department stores as well as toy shops. R. H. White & Co. of Boston published a catalog for the Autumn and Winter of 1884-85. This catalog, now in the Harvard Business School library, contained dolls to tempt you for Christmas presents. Their "French dolls" with bisque heads and jointed composition bodies wearing only a chemise, came in sizes 13, 16½, 19 and 24 inches (33, 42, 48 and 61 cm.) and were priced from $3.75 to $8.25. Dressed "French dolls" in satin costumes were 18 inches (45.5 cm.) for $8.00 and 21 inches (53.5 cm.) for $10.00. While a 15 inch (38 cm.) "French" bisque head, kid body doll dressed in silk and lace cost $5.00.

It is always a question whether dolls advertised as "French" were actually made in France, especially the bisque heads. Some of these may have been made in Germany.

Toward the end of the 19th century, dolls made in America began to appear in Boston stores. Possibly one could buy Izannah Walker cloth dolls and Springfield Wooden dolls in Boston since these dolls were made in nearby New England towns. It is known that the Roxanna Elizabeth McGee Cole cloth dolls, which were made as far away as Arkansas, were sold in the Boston area, according to an 1898 account in the *Boston Advertiser.* Some of these Cole dolls are now in the Wenham Museum in Massachusetts.

Our ancestors enjoyed buying dolls in Boston and now we as collectors can enjoy buying these same dolls that have been cherished through the years, or we can be delighted by seeing them in museums.

Illustration 7. 1870s trade card of Richard Schwarz of Boston. On the back of this card, it mentions that they sell Dolls and Toys. *Coleman Collection.*

Illustration 8. 1870s trade card of Charles Mayer & Co. of Indianapolis, Indiana. Similar dolls would have been sold on Washington Street in Boston. *Coleman Collection.*

The Chocolate Lady or La Belle Chocolatiere

by Ruth E. Whittier

Most doll collectors today are familiar with the half-doll called The Chocolate Lady though there are numerous versions of it. The one that interests us is the one like the 18th century original painting by Jean Etienne Liotard, 1702-1789, Swiss artist. Research shows that the painting was hung in the Dresden Art Gallery in Germany.

The story of its painting by Liotard as given by the late Nita Loving in an early issue of DOLL NEWS (Nov. 1964) is as follows. One cold winter's day back in 1745, a handsome Austrian nobleman, Prince Dietrickstein, stopped at a chocolate shop in Vienna, the first of its kind in the city. The Prince wished to see for himself if this new drink was as good as people claimed. There he met a pretty waitress named Anna Baltauf, daughter of an impoverished knight.

Soon Anna Baltauf became Princess Dietrickstein. For her wedding gift the Prince had her portrait painted by the famous Swiss artist Jean Etienne Liotard who was visiting in Vienna. The artist painted her in a 17th century costume serving chocolate.

It was in the Dresden Gallery that the owner of the Walter Baker Chocolate Company, Henry L. Pierce, found the painting in 1862 and asked permission to have a copy made. Permission given, the painting made, it was brought to the Company offices, then in Dorchester, Mass. It became the trademark for the Walter Baker Chocolate Company, and in 1872 was first used in advertising the Baker products.

One will note in comparing the numerous versions of The Chocolate Lady that those which most closely resemble the Liotard painting wear the rather plain cap, and that the young lady is very erect as she carries her tray of chocolate.

The copy made for the Walter Baker Chocolate Company back in 1862 hung for many years in their offices in Dorchester, being transferred to the new headquarters, when as part of the General Foods Corporation, offices were moved to Dover, Delaware.

We have all known that the Baker Chocolate Company long used The Chocolate Lady in their advertising, on the cans of chocolate, and still do. Imagine my surprise when a

Illustration 1. Lura Sleeper, dressed as she represented the Baker Chocolate Girl. *Photograph by Richard Merrill.*

cousin was visiting me within the last year and showed me pictures of her great-grandmother, my second cousin, a native of Concord, New Hampshire and whom I had known since a small girl, dressed as The Chocolate Lady. It was then I learned that my Cousin Lura Sleeper had been employed by the Walter Baker Chocolate Company back in the 1890s to appear at fairs around the country, and at the World's Fair in Chicago in 1893, as the original live Chocolate Lady in this country. From the profiles of the half-dolls most nearly resembling the Liotard painting, you will note that Lura Sleeper's profile is very close to these half-dolls., My cousin, Lura Sleeper was born August 3, 1872, and died August 14, 1979, having observed her 107th birthday with her family in a New York nursing home. Whether she had a cup of hot chocolate that day, I do not know.

Illustration 2. Half-figure and porcelain painting from the Margaret Woodbury Strong Museum. Reprinted with permission from the *Collector's Encyclopedia of Half-Dolls* by Marion and Werner.

China Half-Figures Called Costume Dolls

by Frieda Marion

Illustration 1. A typical costume doll fashioned from a porcelain half-figure. *Marjorie Stark Collection.* Photograph by Ron Titus.

In the early days of doll collecting, china half-figures were often found with lower cloth bodies and legs, making them full-length dolls. Beautifully dressed in old silks and laces, these charming ladies were called by their owners, costume dolls or period, character or even portrait dolls, the latter because some of the finest examples were believed to resemble famous women of the past.

Illustration #1 shows us a typical costume doll of this type, one of two in the collection of Marjorie Stark. Close examination indicates that the doll was not factory-assembled and dressed, but put together by a previous owner.

The torso is a china half-figure, the model coded MW 147-301 in the Marion/Werner *Collector's Encyclopedia of Half-Dolls.* This is fastened to a hand-made cloth lower body to which are added china legs of the variety usually found on small china-head dolls. The hand-sewn garments include a full-skirted gown made of blue satin ribbon and painted floral decorations, bordered with antique silver lace. Tiny seed pearls encircle the waist and trim the lower edge of the skirt's front panel. Under-

garments are made from fine, lace-trimmed lawn handkerchiefs.

One of the early writers on doll collecting, Janet Pagter Johl, acquaints us with these figures in her book, *More About Dolls,* 1946. She tells about a doll which the owner describes as "most suggestive of ornate Dresden work, although it is not a really old doll" . . . but "was once used on a telephone frame." Scattered through the text are references to dolls which Mrs. Johl classifies as portrait dolls. Some of these, with porcelain torsos, are obviously half-figures originally produced to be fastened to utilitarian objects such as tea-cosies, small lamps, pincushions or frames to hide the old upright telephones!

In a paragraph on "misrepresentation," the author tells about a pincushion purchased at auction for a quarter (those days have gone, alas!). Later, the porcelain top, again termed Dresden, was removed from the pincushion, attached to a cloth body and costumed and sold for what was then considered a high price. This practice of altering a pincushion top to make a full-length doll was denounced by one collector as "atrocious." Nevertheless, it probably explains the origin of many of the so-called costume dolls found in early collections.

Mrs. Johl also writes about a "delicate, lovely doll" with a fine porcelain torso on a pressed-paper lower body. The owner's detailed account and the accompanying illustration lead us to conclude that the doll in question was a marked Dressel and Kister half-figure, from the company's outstanding Medieval series. It's interesting that collectors are apt to describe these costume dolls as Dresden or Meissen, although many of them seem to be half-figures manufactured by the Dressel and Kister company situated in Passau.

In her later book, *Still More About Dolls*, 1950, Mrs. Johl shows us two other examples of these half-figures assembled and dressed. One is termed a "French telephone doll with Meissen head and hands," said to have been brought to this country from Paris in 1887, possibly a bit early for the ubiquitous telephone covers. Perhaps the assembly, with its very wide skirt, was actually intended to be a tea-cosie.

The other doll pictured was called "Sarah Siddons" after the famous British actress, Sarah Kemble Siddons (1755-1831). Coded MW 108-501 in the Marion/Werner *Encyclopedia,* the model is claimed to have a striking resemblance to a miniature on the lid of an antique patch box which was signed with Mrs. Siddon's name. The model is a familiar one to half-doll collectors, but not having seen the portrait on the patch box, we can't make judgement on the likeness. Colemans' *Collector's Encyclopedia of Dolls* states that the Dressel and Kister company was founded in 1841.

We now know that many of the quality Dressel and Kister models were factory-assembled with wire-reinforced bodies and specially designed porcelain legs, as shown here in illustrations #2 and #4. These elegant pincushions, powder-boxes or jewel cases were so elaborately fashioned that they easily may have impressed early doll collectors as being noteworthy for the costumed dolls alone.

Research has also verified the conjecture of the 1940's that some fine half-figures were actually designed as portraits of famous women, as seen in our illustration #5.

In the early part of this century half-figures were the decorator's delight, but wars and changing attitudes toward home furnishings wiped out the craze for topping countless household objects with china half-figures. Yet the little porcelain torsos were so appealing that many doll collectors who stumbled across them, found them irresistable. It's understandable that, not being certain of their origin, these collectors chose to fashion the finer half-figures into full-length dolls and costume them with loving care, and then, of course, display them on the shelves beside their antique dolls.

Costume or portrait dolls, whatever name was given them, we like to think that they still belong among our collections today.

Illustration 5. A true portrait half-doll, this delicate torso was modeled to represent Marie Antoinette (1755-93). A painting by Mme Elizabeth Vigee-Lebrun inspired the unknown modeler who carefully reproduced the tragic young Queen's fashionable hair style and beruffled bodice in fine porcelain. *Dorothy Burton Collection. Photograph by Jim Schlessenger.*

Illustration 2. A quality porcelain half-doll factory-assembled and mounted on pincushion box with matching decoration. Jointed at shoulders with right arm positioned to hold gold-braid basket, the doll is beautifully dressed in delicate silks, laces and gold trim, with sheer muslin undergarments. *Barbara Schilde Collection. Photograph by Jim Zeitz.*

Illustration 3. This model is the torso used in the assembly shown in *Illustration #2.* Here we see the shoulder joints and the right arm modeled to hold a basket of fruit or flowers. Some of these torsos were apparently sold to be assembled at home by the buyer. *Charlotte Bill Collection. Photograph by Gene Tuck.*

Illustration 4. Another Dressel and Kister porcelain half-doll made into a full-length seated figure, exquisitely costumed in silk, lace, ribbons and gold trim. Period dolls was one of the terms early collectors used to classify these fastidious ladies. *Jim Fernando Collection. Photograph by Norma Werner.*

2½'' Silver half-doll on beige velvet pincushion. Hallmarks on head ''C.S. & F.S., anchor, lion passant, date letter, No. 586½''. Made in Birmingham, England, 1863. Over all height 6''. *Elizabeth MacMahon Donoghue Collection. Photograph by Richard Merrill.*

LADY HALF-FIGURE. 6'' half-doll, china to waist, made into 15½'' doll. Brown molded hair with brush marks, combed into a high bun, horizontal curls at sides, with spilling curls at the back. Features are delicately painted. She is beautifully costumed in a handmade pink silk dress with embroidered lace overlay skirt and flowered ribbon. White china legs with pink painted bows at the knees and pink flat-soled shoes complete this lovely doll. *Eleanor Harriman Collection. Photograph by Richard Merrill.*

Market vignette, figures and accessories are 18th century terra cotta, wood, wax and various materials. Figures sculpted by G. Gori and A. Viva.

The Presepio Figure and Environment

by Frank L. Hanley and
Jeffery G. Gueno
Photography by the Authors from their Collection

In Medieval Church Latin - - "praesepe"; in Italian - - "Presepio"; in English - - "Crib"; in German - - "Krippe"; in Portuguese - - "Belem"; in Spanish - - "Nacimiento"; in French - - "Crèche"

With the beginning of the 17th century the making of presepi had become a recognized trade in Naples, and the artists and craftsmen engaged in it were commonly known as "Figurari." Among the most famous of these pioneers were: Vaccaro, Falcone, and Somma. Crib figures, generally known as "Pastori," were becoming a little world to themselves. The earliest Neapolitan cribs had all been fixed groups of statues; but a new technique was introduced when Vaccaro made a set of figures for the church, Santa Maria in Portici, which were dressed in stuff clothes.

From that moment on, the Figurari tended to discard the solid figure in favor of the puppet-type with an articulated wood body or a body of rags or oakum wound on wire, and feet, hands and head exquisitely modeled, either of wood or terra cotta. The finish of

Illustration 1. 18th century Neapolitan shepherd with harp, polychrome terra cotta head, wood hands and feet. 11 inches tall. Sculpted by Lorenza Mosca.

every tiny detail was accentuated when the Figurari became empolyed in the china factory of Capo di Monte, presently in Naples. Some of the Figurari were invited to work in Spain, taking with them Italian models, bringing back Spanish ones. When a Neapolitan king married a Saxon princess there came in designs from the Meissen factory, and again other Figurari found work in Germany.

Under the guidance and enthusiasm of Kings Carlo III and Ferdinando IV, the Presepio quickly became a genre picture of Neapolitan life; often as theatrical as any Mystery Play.

What can the hobby of the Kings not do? It was the fancy of Carlo III of Naples that brought about the spread of crèche art in Naples, then Italy, and finally north in the Alps, in Germany and Austria. Ascending the throne in 1739, his two Sicilys - - so was his country called at that time, encompassed the island as well as Naples. All artists and artisans were set to work on the execution of figures, buildings and backgrounds; especially the porcelain artists of Capo di Monte.

This, the 18th cenutry Neapolitan Presepio or Crèche, is one of the most particularly grandiose self-representations that we know of from the 18th century. Without a doubt, these are great works of art, and are very reliable sources or treasuries for the researcher.

18th century Naples was extremely important as a major port and center of trade. As such, it was an extremely wealthy city. Its Bourbon rulers made the city a flourishing center for artists and craftsmen of all fields. One of the most fascinating of art forms patronized by these rulers, particularly by King Ferdinand IV and his Queen Maria Carolina, was the Presepio. King Ferdinand himself is said to have carved figures and Maria Carolina and her ladies whiled away many hours fashioning intricate costumes that are miniature reproductions of dress seen in the southern regions of Italy, court costume, and exotic dress from far away lands. Nobles and merchants often competed with each other in lavish Presepio displays, probably hoping to capture the King's favorable attention.

Illustration 2. Portrait-type Calabrian woman by Lorenzo Mosca. Costume and fabrics of the very finest quality. 18th century Neapolitan. 15 inches tall.

Truly, it would almost appear that the Neapolitans believed Christ to have been born among the people of southern Italy and surrounded their Nativity displays with scenes of everyday occupations and settings found in 18th century Naples.

Illustration 3. 18th century Neapolitan female tarentella dancer by G. Gori. Costume and fabrics are original and of exceptional quality. 16 inches tall.

Illustration 4. Alfresco dining scene using 18th century figures and accessories of terra cotta, wood, wax, glass and various materials. Figures by Celebrand and Bottiglieri.

Illustration 5. Central nativity group housed in a cabinet 10½ feet by 6½ feet deep. All figures and accessories 17th and 18th century Neapolitan.

To those of us accustomed to crèche scenes comprised of the Holy Family, ox and ass, perhaps a few shepherds and sheep, the three wise men and, of course, at least one angel, the mature 18th century Neapolitan Crèche is overwhelming.

Street vendors peddle hundreds of small foodstuffs and general household wares made of wood, terra cotta or wax. Minstrels play their instruments for the amusement of the passersby. Inn guests eat heartily; citizens shop or gamble; wealthy citizens mingle on the street with the peasantry. All are adorned with nearly every item of clothing, nearly every accessory in use at that time.

Though the earliest figures were crudely carved of wood, few of them remain. Most of the surviving figures are from the period of highest development in the late 17th and 18th centuries, when the most prominent sculptors were responsible for the marvelous character studies represented in the scenes.

The late 17th century wood figures have heads, hands and feet of finely carved wood on a wood articulated body. These figures should not be confused with the late 18th and 19th centuries wood figures from Mexico and Spain, which are usually painted blue on the torso. The Italian and German figures of wood were rarely painted beyond the knee, elbow and upper chest.

Illustration 7. 17th century Italian polychrome wood, 18 inches tall, fully jointed; silk, gold braid, semi-precious stones, solid silver censer.

At an unknown date these wood bodies were eliminated in favor of the more versatile hemp and oakum over wire armature while still retaining the wood head, lower arms and legs. The aesthetic quality found in these early wood figures cannot easily be described, analogous to the quiet sophistication of the early Queen Anne dolls.

In the 1st quarter of the 18th century, when terra cotta was introduced as the sculpture material for the heads, regardless of other advantages, the versatile plasticity of the medium gave the sculptor more freedom of line, elaborate detail capabilities, and allowed for superb realism in the Baroque tradition.

Illustration 6. 18th century Neapolitan figure of Joseph with an exceptional head and chestplate. 18 inches tall.

The terra cotta and wood are covered with gesso priming, underpainted with tempera color and finished with an oil resin glaze. The wire armature of the bodies allows the figures to be posed in postures as expressive as their features.

Though it is known that many of the finer figures in Neapolitan scenes are portraits of donors and the like, it is easy to understand that since Naples was an important trade seaport, many strange peoples were brought to its shores. Thus, without a doubt, these Turkish sea robbers, Moors, Spaniards and Africans were the silent and unknowing models for the Wisemen from the East and their exotic following.

It is difficult to decide what is more awesome, the variety and multiplicity of figures and accessories surviving from so long ago and their beauty, or completely harmonious settings which look so in keeping with their contents that it is difficult to realize that the general image of a Neapolitan Crèche figure is but a solitary figure on a plain stand with no visible accessory with which it was intended. Similar to children's playthings (dolls and toys), the artistic merits of Crèche figures do allow the figure to stand alone in any general collection, without accessory or environment.

After careful research and study of this Baroque idiom, authentic and very rare figures, which have survived from that period, have been collected and assembled in Lafayette, Louisiana over the past 18 years.

Illustration 8. 18th century female figure by Celebrano, original Calabrian costume. 16 inches tall.

Illustration 9. Grouping of 18th century Neapolitan figures from the Magi entourage. Included are rare accessories of various metals, leather and wood.

Illustration 10. Close-up of an 18th century bagpipe player. Terra cotta head with unusual modeling of cheeks and mouth. 18 inches tall.

Bibliography

Berliner, Rudolph, *Die Weihnachtskrippe* (Prestel Verlag, Munich, 1955)

Borrelli, Gennaro, *The Wood Sculpture in Neapolitan Presepio Figures of the 17th Century* (San Vitale, Bologna, 1974)

Borrelli, Gennaro *Il Presepe Napoletano* (Luca D'Agostino, 1970)

Borrelli, Gennaro, *Sanmartino* (Falsto Fiorentino, Naples, 1966)

Bruckmann, Verlag F., *Buntes Krippenbuchlein* (F. Bruckmann, Munich, 1957)

Catello, Elio, *Francesco Celebrano* (Arturo Berisio, Naples, 1969)

De Robeck, Nesta, *The Christmas Crib* (Bruce Pub. Co., Milwaukee, 1956)

(Enal Dopalavoro), Il Presepe (Naples)

Felkel, Erwin, *Krippen* (Sudwest Verlag, Munich, 1970)

Heidrich, Ricarda, *Zur Krippe her Kommet* (Union Verlag, Stuttgart, 1965)

Mancini, Franco, *Il Presepe* Napoletano (Sandea/Sansoni)

(Palazzo Real) *Figure Presepi ali Napoletane Dal Sec. XIV al XVII* (Naples, 1970)

Parrilli, Mario, *Civilta della Campania* (anno 1-N.1-Salerno, 1970)

Picone, Marina, *Presepi a San Martino* (L'arte Tipografica, Naples, 1964)

Ringler, Josef, *Alte Tiroler Weihnachtskrippen* (Universitatsverlag Wagner, Innsbruck - - Munich, 1972)

Zeichnungen/Hansmann, Claus, *Krippen* (Bayerisches Nationalmuseum, Munich, 1972)

Zeppegno, Luciano, *Presepi, Artistici & Popolari* (Instituto Geografico de Agostini, Novara)

We hesitate giving any restoration techniques due to any potential over-zealousness and also to the obstacles one may encounter in such an endeavor. However, here are a few suggestions which may apply to many wood and terra cotta figures, either Crèche, religious or even many standard wooden dolls.

Material needed:
small soft bristle artist brushes
small squares of cotton fabric
1/2 cup water
a few drops of ammonia
oil of poppy or walnut (art supply stores)
round toothpicks
cotton swabs
patience

This procedure was demonstrated and outlined for us in Naples, Italy on a research trip a few years ago.

It is imperative that liquids do not come in contact with any part of the costume, as damage of some sort will likely occur. On some figures and dolls, fabric may at least be gently slid aside. If this cannot be done easily then perhaps some wrapping of the fabric areas with paper toweling, secured with tape, might aid in some protection.

The head and extremities are to be cleaned with a cotton swab dampened in the ammonia-water solution, working very gently in circular motions, being most careful around surface cracks and raised areas of paint. Clean small areas at a time, drying carefully with the cotton fabric as you proceed.

Continue until the entire head or extremity is cleaned and free of surface dirt (Some will always remain, do not over clean, the finish may come off before some dirt).

The glass eyes may be cleaned with the rounded toothpick, crushed slightly on the end, and dampened slightly with the ammonia-water mixture. Use *no* real pressure in swabbing out the fixed soil on the glass.

Finally you *sparingly* apply either of the oils, letting this stand for an hour or so. Then lightly and carefully buff with clean white cotton on the end of a finger, in a circular motion, again paying special attention to damaged and raised areas. This oiling will restore some of the luster to the surface and will aid the protective coats of varnish or size used on these figures of terra cotta or wood.

Strong Museum Woodens

11½'' wooden peg-jointed doll front view; hair carved with random grooves and painted in curls on temples and sides of neck in dark brown, eyes painted blue as well as shoes and scallop line at top of corset, prominent carving of pushed-up breasts and of calf muscles in legs, but no ankle bones, and shoes with pointed toes show very little shaping and no heels, detailed carving of ears and nose with deep nostrils.

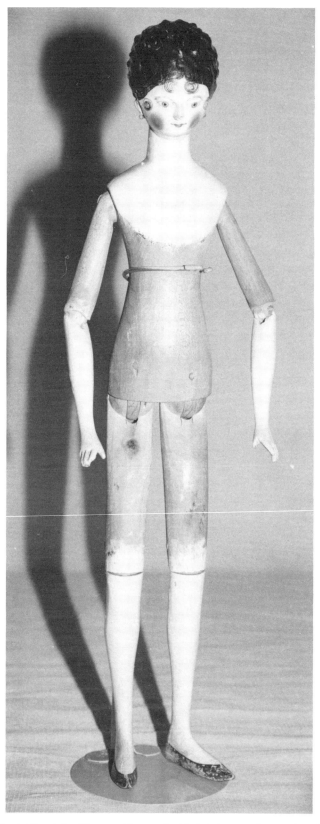

Illustration 1. 21" wooden doll with carved 'porcupine' hairstyle, prominent painted blue eyes, long feet with painted green shoes with wedge heel, outlined in black.

Wooden Dolls of 1795-1815: A Time of Paradox

by Estelle L. Johnston

The dates are somewhat arbitrary - as many dates must necessarily be - but are representative of a brief stylistic period in the history of wooden dolls. The particular dolls under examination range in size, in facial type, and in hair treatment, but all share a similarity of exposed carved ears and carved shoes with pointed toes and low wedge-shaped heels, all usually outlined in black and imitating an actual style of shoe seen within these dates. My thesis is that these dolls not only differ obviously from the so-called Queen Anne dolls still being made in this era, but differ significantly from their immediate offspring, the tuck comb or common peg-wooden types.

The French Revolution accelerated a hitherto gentle fashion movement and marked the beginnings of a radical change of taste from opulent rococo to neoclassicism, to slender airy lightness and to what is appropriately termed the *vertical epoch.* Certainly one of the first impressions one gets of these dolls is of a vertical stylistic slenderness which correlates absolutely with the new forms in furniture and architecture of the time - a style enjoying renewed appreciation in our own time for its understated elegance. There is a noticeable quality of carving in these wooden dolls which has its heritage in the carving of religious figures for churches and shrines, and in the European love of puppets and marionettes, while the method of jointing is identical to that of artists' lay figures or mannikins in use from Renaissance days. And, most interestingly, the dolls of this brief period are usually individual and highly artistic in their conception and execution, ranging from an exactness close to portraiture to a surprisingly subtle and humorous caricature of the period.

These were times of a return to gaiety after the reign of terror and of the guillotine - gaiety in spite of the comings and goings of Napoleon. Woman looked to Paris for her style. And the style was Greco-Roman as in sandals for the feet, sheer drapings in tunic effect for the body, loose curls bound with ribbons or braids wound vaguely a la Grecque for the head. These would prove both too impractical and too informal. For the new Empire, a new version of the classical was required and found: sheer white or light-colored dresses which could be 'dressed up' with velvet train for court or colored silk spencer for the street, low almost heelless slippers, close bonnets covering the head in helmet fashion. The waistline was as high as it could go under a pushed-up bosom to create a long slim column, with hair cut short or dressed close to the head. In the mood we now call backlash, a red ribbon round the throat and a 'ceinture a la Victime' seemed morbidly amusing . . . or hair chopped short a la porc-épic, like those who had been polled for execution.[1] As this first decade passed the simplicity of the clothing changed into a caricature of its own, loaded down with ruffles and puffings, rouleaux and fluffings as the human mind took flight from the (by now) too well-known world of antiquity into the imagined romance of the Middle Ages.[2] "Sense giving way to sensibility" brought about a new adoration of woman as angel and, as it must always, produced its own paradoxes - in fact and in fashion. As woman has so often done throughout history, the lady of the new nineteenth century flirted with masculine styles; a jockey cap here, a military swag there - a raffishness in amusing contradiction to the ridiculously frilled and fragile angel.

Dancing became a mania and the "lewd, lascivious German dance, the waltz" . . . the Imperial Waltz imported from the Rhine and beloved of Vienna held sway in 1815 despite protests from such as Byron![3]

> The early nineteenth century created a chasm in the European mind . . . (between) the new middle classes nourished by the Industrial Revolution . . . hopeful and energetic, but without a scale of values . . . sandwiched between a corrupt aristocracy and a brutalised poor (which) produced a defensive morality, conventional, complacent, hypocritical; and the finer spirits - poets, painters, novelists - heirs of the Romantic movement (were) haunted by disaster . . . cut off from the prosperous majority.[4]

Another paradox: the burgeoning bourgeoisie versus the Romantic ideal.

These were the times in which these particular dolls were conceived and created. And it is truly extraordinary that in the Gröden Tal, relatively remote and independent, alternately claimed by Austria and Italy, scarcely touched by Napoleon as he marched through Italy and back into Austria, wood

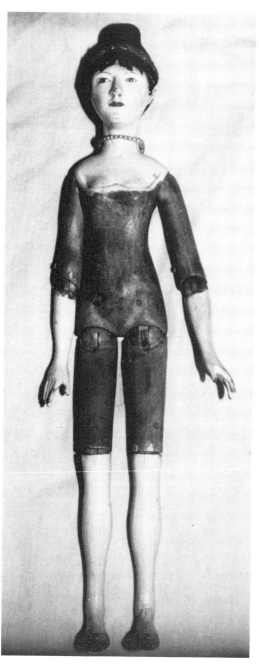

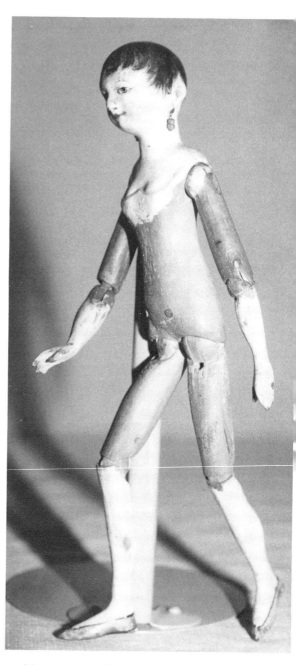

Illustration 2. 15½'' wooden doll with high realism, carved hair with carved and painted decorations, corset line at bosom, wonderful pink shoes with carved trim on vamp.

Illustration 3. 10'' wooden doll with painted 'porcupine' hair, painted grey eyes, identical corset line carved on bosom, gold shoes with narrow wedge heel in white.

carvers captured so exquisitely the paradoxes and humours of their own time. I embarked on a long search to pin down the Gröden Tal (valley) extending east and west along the Gröden River, which is approximately thirty miles south of the Brenner Pass and west of Cortina (site of Winter Games in the '60's) in the now Italian Dolomites - consequently renamed Val Gardena. In the nineteenth century the town of St. Ulrich (now Ortisei) was a chief tourist resort, but it is difficult to imagine anyone traveling for pleasure before railroads! To be sure, Napoleon slogged it with his armies, and mountain people were traditionally and of necessity mobile in pursuit of their livestock if not their living . . . but surely not the fashionable folk.

Winter photographs show towns nestled between the hills under thick blankets of snow, very similar to the small Austrian villages a little farther north. One imagines the talented wood carvers of this region whittling the long winters away. In *Kinderspielzeug aus alter Zeit* by Karl Grober and Julianne Metzger

"Apart from Nurnberg in the second half of the eighteenth century there arose a new center in the South Tirol in Grödner Tal, with St. Ulrich as its center, for the toy industry. As early as 1643 a wood carver, Christian Trebinger from St. Jakob is mentioned. The inhabitants of the Grödner Tal are very good at languages. Almost all speak three languages (Ladin is their main language) and because of this they have conducted their business and trade from the very beginning. Many Grödner wares were carried in baskets from door to door; it is said these pedlars travelled as far as Lisbon and Russia. Also, in the the Grödner Tal, they were foremost carvers of crucifixes and then doll makers. Still today many are, at least as a sideline, sculptors, turners or carvers. From there stems the saying:

"the form is contained within the wood, man merely removes the excess"

About 1823 Steffen Keez reported: here in the Grödner Tal are manifold carved goods of pine, often indeed works of sculpture, and the Tirol work overall is on a par with that of the Berchtolsgadener. "The number of workers since 1780 has increased tenfold. There is a carver in every house. A design establishment was founded in 1822 in St. Ulrich. There is still today a museum and even a carvers' school. From time immemorial the Grödnertalers have been amused by caricature. Alas they are, owing to requests from abroad, swinging to that extreme and providing almost exclusively rather exaggerated caricatures and grotesquely distorted figures."[5.]

This is a significant passage because the few examples of this type of doll I have been able to see and photograph show the individuality of carving moving from realistic representation to highly stylized spoof of the prevailing fashion, and the trend to further grotesquerie is not hard to imagine. One could also say that 1822, with the establishment of design control in St. Ulrich, heralded the end of originality.

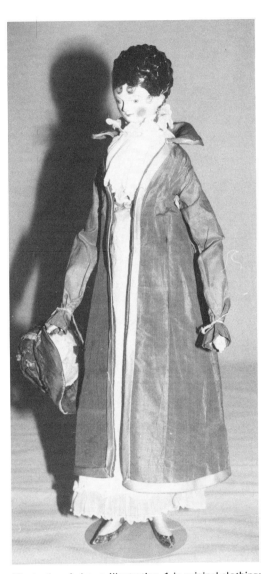

Illustration 4 shows Illustration 1 in original clothing: linen shift, cotton tunic dress with sheer hand-embroidered frill at hem, green silk coat trimmed with ivory silk, matching green silk bonnet.

Illustration 6 shows close-up of Illustration 2 with portrait head and great diginity.

Illustration 7 shows remarkable similarity between Illustration 3 and period painting. Ingres' portrait of Mlle. Riviere in the Louvres.

As far as we know, then, these dolls were made for a relatively brief time before the even more elongated and conventionally stylized peg-jointed dolls known as tuck combs became the standard fare. Although the move into romanticism was well-established by the 1820's, the taste for the vertical line continued in these wooden dolls and was literally solidified by the early papier-mâchés on their slim kid bodies with long but unjointed wooden limbs. But neither the "tuck combs" nor the "milliner's models" have the flair for realism or the tongue-in-cheek wit of the early jointed wood dolls. In addition to the excellent carving and painting of the heads - which convinces me that the hand that carved also attended to the painting - there is usually some carving of corset or fichu at the bosom, the fingers are realistic and well delineated, and the lower legs are positively and particularly winsome. Sometimes they concentrate on realistic calf muscles, or rather prominent ankle bones,

or long and faintly ridiculous feet (the prevailing style with pointed toe and low flat heel is not becoming to the average foot, and some of us remember an equally unflattering revival in this century). The torso is carved in the ideal shape produced in part by the long stays of that period: gently curved with not much variation between the natural waist and the hip to create a smooth progression from bosom to bootline. When found with original clothing, it is thin and simple, cotton or soft silk with cotton or linen shift but no drawers.

A brief period of unique and wonderful dolls, particularly satisfying to hold in the hand and to move, for, as the *Encyclopedia of World Art* says,

> "to move dolls, to make them walk and sit, and to dress and undress them satisfies an urge for dynamic mimesis."[6].

We can only regret that there are not more and rejoice in the few examples surviving for us today.

FOOTNOTES:

1. *Dress and Society 1560-1970,* Geoffrey Squire, Viking Press, 1974, p. 133
2. Ibid., p. 148
3. Ibid., p. 142
4. *Civilization,* Kenneth Clark, Harper & Row, 1969, p. 316
5. *Kinderspielzeug aus alter Zeit,* Karl Grober and Julianne Metzger, Edition Leipzig, Germany 1965, first printed 1929, p. 34 (loosely translated by ELJ)
6. *Encyclopedia of World Art,* Vol. VI, McGraw-Hill, 1962, col. 5

NOTES:

Books showing photographs of these early jointed wooden dolls:
Children's Toys of Yesterday, C. Geoffrey Holme, London 1932, p. 29
Dolls, Antonia Fraser, reprinted 1973 but still incorrectly captioned, p. 31 #46
A Taste of Honey, Marlowe Cooper & Dee Van Kampen, California 1976, p. 47
The Collector's Book of Dolls' Clothes, Coleman, Crown Pub. 1975, p. 33 #37 and p. 40 #50 and #51
Handbook of Collectible Dolls, Merrill & Perkins, Vol. 3, p. 224Q, copyright 1977 by Madeline Merrill and Richard Merrill; shows an interesting variant with carved necklace at swivel-joint neck and painted skull ?for wig
Doll Collectors Manual 1973, p. 61
Doll Collectors Manual 1964, pp. 40-44 #19, #24, #25 and the whole fascinating article, *The Decline and Fall of the Wooden Doll,* Ruth E. and R. C. Mathes

Illustration 5 shows profile of Illustration 1 emphasizing the zany caricuture aspect; new jade earrings perched on original wire loops for effect.

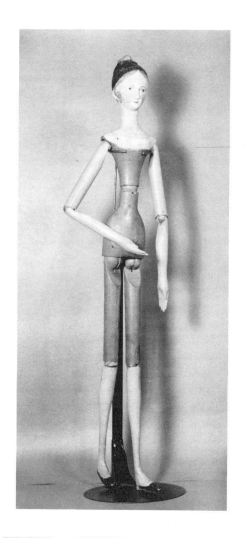

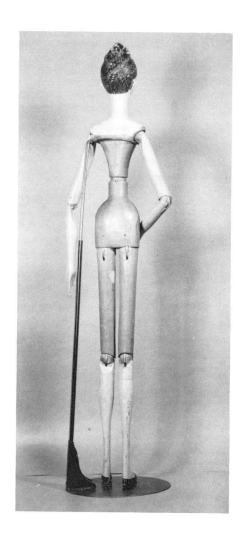

Swivel Waist Wood

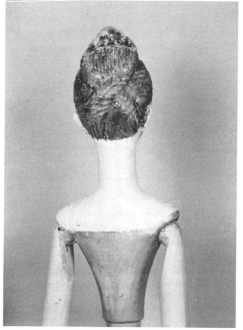

Unusually large, 32 inch, fully jointed early wooden. Note the jointed waistline. Hair style has carved comb, surrounded by carved and painted braid. From the collection of the late Estelle Winthrop.

The Story of Miss Betsy and Her Doll

by Marion Ball Poe

A genteel Quaker lady known to her family and friends as Miss Betsy is the heroine of this story.

Elizabeth Waln Wistar was the oldest child of Mary Waln and Thomas Wistar of Philadelphia, Pennsylvania. She was born in 1788 and died in 1880, at the age of 92 years.

Elizabeth never married, but had the responsibility of rearing two nephews after the death of a younger sister. The boys were T. Wistar Brown and Moses Brown, Jr.

The family business was located on Market Street, above 10th, and listed in the Philadelphia City Directory as Wistar and Cook, Merchants. It is interesting to note that when Mr. Wistar received an order for rifles, he refused to sell such an item and retired from business.

Prior to this time the family believes he sold beautiful glass tableware and window glass made by his famous brother, Casper Wistar, in his glass factory in Salem, New Jersey.

This bit of family history is to support my story of this doll, also known as Miss Betsy.

The doll was willed to Elizabeth's nephew, T. Wistar Brown, who became the grandfather of my friend, Margaret Morton Creese, and it was from her that I received the doll.

Mrs. Creese, wife of Dr. James Creese, President of Drexel University, (where I graduated), knowing my interest in antique dolls, offered to sell me this doll. She had found the family heirloom in an old trunk when preparing to move.

I made a hurried trip from Pittsburgh, Pennsylvania to her home on June 23, 1957 to see the doll, Miss Betsy. What a thrilling moment it was when Dr. Creese placed the beautiful doll in my lap! Mrs. Creese gave me many interesting facts concerning her Quaker family and later sent me a copy of the Wistar family tree, to substantiate the history of the doll.

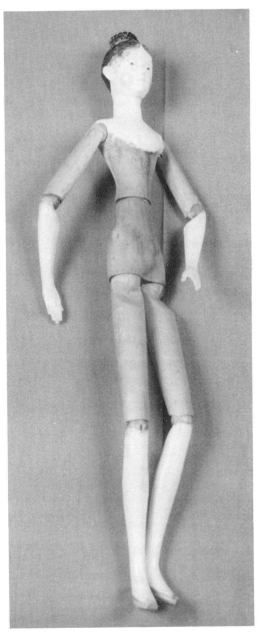

Illustration 1. 32 inch wooden doll with eight ball and socket joints and a midriff swivel joint. Note carved hair with braid, trimmed with a yellow band. Circa 1800-1810.

We assume the doll was the only toy Miss Betsy owned and cherished as she kept it in such pristine condition. She had no time to play with dolls in her busy home life.

The following day I had an appointment with Mr. Bart Anderson, at the Chester County Historical Society, in West Chester, Pennsylvania. When I showed him my doll he was amazed to see a doll similar to one in his collection.

My rare wooden doll, called Miss Betsy, is 32 inches tall, circa 1800. She has eight ball and socket joints; shoulders, elbows, hips and knees, plus a most unique midriff swivel joint. Her painted black hair is hand carved to simulate a short hairdo, with center part and beautiful brush curls around her face. A crown or coronet braid is featured on top of her head, with a yellow band trim. She has a long, narrow neck and high bosom, painted in flesh color. She has pink cheeks, brown painted eyes and large ears. There are two brass loops remaining in her ears where drop earrings were once attached but, we assume, were removed by her Quaker owner. Her face, arms (elbows to finger tips), legs (knees to toes) are painted in enamel finish. Her low cut shoes are painted pink, with stub toes. Her unpainted body is in natural wood finish and is in excellent condition for her age.

The only mark on this doll is a number five, written in script, at the center of the back hip. To identify the source of this doll, I refer to an article by Ruth and R. C. Mathes in *Doll Collectors' Manual, 1964.* They suggest that this type wooden doll was produced by master craftsmen of the city guilds in the Grödner Tal in the Bavarian and Austrian Tyrol.

Mrs. Creese believes this doll might have been purchased in Germany when Elizabeth's father was on a buying trip, or he may have acquired it from an importer of toys in Philadelphia about 1800-1810.

When Dorothy Coleman visited me on July 20, 1976, she admired the doll and said it would be late 18th century, the doll being older than her clothes.

If you refer to the photos of the doll's costume, you will see the style and workmanship used for these various pieces of clothing. No doubt the costume was made by Elizabeth Wistar in her later years, after her early training in handwork at home and school. Young girls were taught to sew, to make fine clothing and household items. She might have had help from the family dressmaker who was a visitor in the family home on seasonal dates. (A suggestion by Margaret Creese.)

The most beautiful and interesting item in her wardrobe is her dress of homespun linen. Tiny hand stitches adorn this handsome white dress of the Empire period. A long, full skirt, 18 inches, is gathered to a fitted bodice, which features one-inch tiny vertical tucks across the front of the blouse to produce fullness. A small casing at the top of the blouse has a cord within the hem for a draw string to adjust this fullness to proper position. A very unusual fitted inner lining of facing attached to the inside of the bodice holds the gathered front bodice in place against the doll's chest, producing a high bust line, and beautiful effect. The long, full, set-in sleeves are gathered at the shoulder with cording technique used for trim. The sleeves are finished with a deep cuff with a ruffle at the top of the cuff, made of the same material. Tiny tapes are used to fasten this garment at the rear opening.

A shift or chemise of mid-calf length is made of two pieces of white linen with fell seams at the sides, rolled edges around the sleeves and hemline and a deep oval neckline with bias seam binding finishing the edge. The sleeves are short, with gussets applied under the arms for ease and fullness.

The doll wears a half petticoat, gathered to a waistband, with center back opening, very plain in design. The outer, fancy petticoat is made of fine white linen fabric. It has a full skirt, trimmed with three graduated tucks above the hemline. This skirt is attached to a band-type bodice, with shaped underarm sections. White one-quarter inch tapes attached to the top of the bodice go over the top of the doll's shoulders. A tiny hem across the front and back of the bodice contains a tape to draw up the fullness, and two tapes at the rear tie the petticoat at the opening.

The leglets, knee-length pants, are two tubular pieces of very sheer white fabric, finished at the top by a tiny hem containing a tiny tape as draw string to tie the leglet to the knee of the doll. The leglets are trimmed with broderie anglaise, a decorative edging made in Switzerland and very popular for childrens' clothes. A band of this beautiful white embroidery is attached to the bottom of the gathered leglet.

You will note in picture #2 that the doll is wearing two blue ribbon rosettes that she won at an exhibit. Each ribbon rosette has a picture of a doll head painted in the center of the button, one of which is a likeness of my wooden doll, Miss Betsy.

The Wistar family had later moved to Germantown, a section of Philadelphia and were members of the Quaker Meeting. Miss Betsy was evidently exhibited at a bazaar held at this Quaker Meeting. We assume the doll was dressed prior to this exhibit. Quakers had annual functions and exhibited excellent handwork.

We are thankful that the doll passed through several generations and was preserved for a future doll collector who carried the doll from Pennsylvania in 1967 to Marion's and Miss Betsy's new home in Peabody, Kansas.

Illustration 3. Picture illustrates individual pieces of clothing worn by Miss Betsy. Two blue ribbon rosettes.

39

Inclination of the Age

by Frank L. Hanley and Jeffery G. Gueno

Illustration 1.

About the shallow games which occupy our age
Let us not look upon them with contempt
Under more sophisticated guise or posings
They are also our lot.

The above shown translation of the platitude which accompanies this distinctive doll intriguingly ties in with the irony of the catalogue* text of a very important auction of Friday, April 19, 1974, (code name "Padouk") which reads as follows:

Lot number 107 *"Another Queen Anne Papier-Mâché Doll."*

---

*Sotheby and Company

The catalogue described her in these terms: The head with painted features, the papier-mâché body with wooden hands, the legs hinged at the hips and knees and with metal hooks to keep the legs straight; wearing her original nun's habit consisting of two white shifts, a white wool habit and scapular with a black veil and a white wimple and a brown wool cloak, wearing white stockings and leather shoes, 1710-1720, 17½ inches high.

*** The habit is that of a choir nun of the Benedictine order.

The title of the engraving is "The Portrait of a Daughter of M. Mahon with Doll Dressed as a Nun" engraved by P. L. Surugne in 1743.

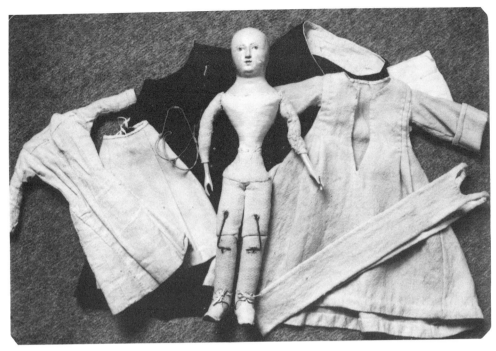

Illustration 2.

It was the property of Henry d'Allemagne in Paris.

Let us examine the amount of detail worked into this doll's costume. The white stockings mentioned in the catalogue text are, more correctly, part of the entire body covering and the fabric is 18th Century homespun cotton in an overshot weave. All seams are sewn together with heavy linen thread.

The chemise of tightly woven coarse linen, has two English style gores on either side of the skirt and a gusset under each arm. The neck opening, without a drawstring and virtually free of any ornamentation, has the points folded forward and stitched to the face of the fabric to give the appearance of a yoke. The sleeves are simply cuffed.

The second shift, actually the petticoat skirt made of homespun wool twill with ties in the back, is pleated in contrary fashion from center-front and bound with a delicate linen band. The habit itself, made of the same twill, is cut like the *Robe Gattante* or sacque. Its back pleats are fuller and deeper than those in front. The dress opens in the front to just below the waist level where it is closed by pins. The sleeves are full with wide, turned back cuffs. The neck opening of the habit is handsomely faced with top grade linen and all seams are French or flat felled. The scapular, constructed of identical wool twill and possessing a neck opening bound again with fine linen, is completely hemmed with slip-stitch. The wimple, all blind hemmed, is made of high quality linen. The sheer black wool veil is faced with white linen and finished with fine-corded, piped seams. The circular cloak is of dark brown felted wool 1/8 inch thick. Its neck is bound with heavy black linen, closed with cord ties, and monogrammed with the letters K.A.

Although the quiet beauty of this doll is enhanced by the aforementioned costume, its uniqueness lies in its softly rounded face and liquid painted eyes. A remarkable feature of the doll's head is the use of definite wire loops at the ears. Most importantly, however, is the fact that this Queen Anne doll is one of the few of its type remaining with original costume and construction totally intact.

Much has been written previously on carton dolls, consequently only a description of her costume was necessary here as she is of the earlier carton type of the 18th Century. This means that she is of a modeled grey paper pulp and binder. Her head and torso are one, with only the separate articulated and latched legs of carton. She has the usual rolled linen upper arm and lower arm of wood, which is typical of Queen Anne dolls.

This type of carton should never be confused with the later, 19th Century more primitive type or with any composition materials which are sometimes defined as carton.

41

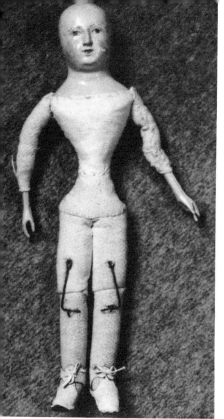

Illustration 3.

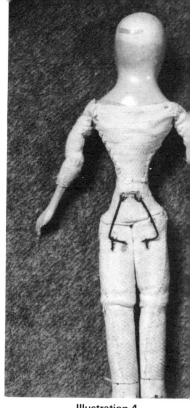

Illustration 4.

Illustration 5.

Illustration 6.

Illustration 7.

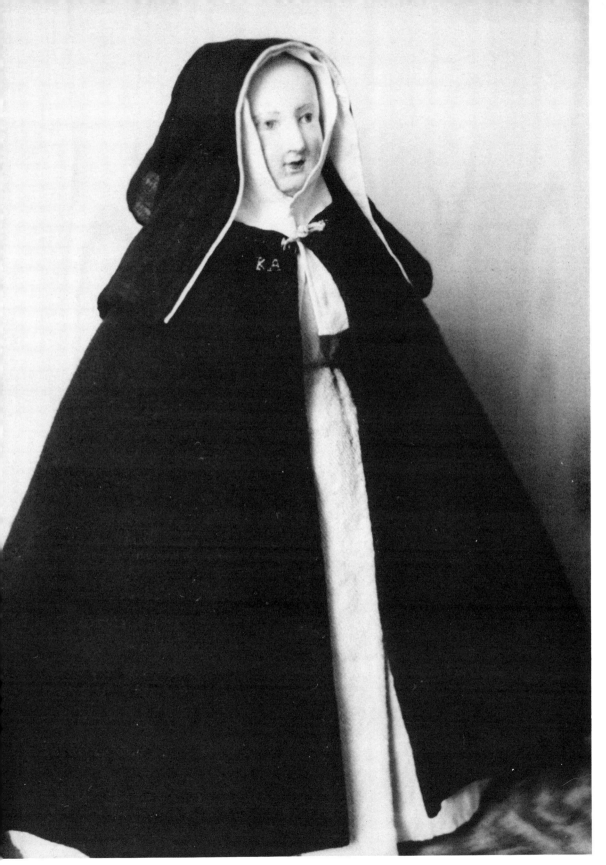

Illustration 8.

Portraits in Papier-Mâché

by Lorna Lieberman
Photography by Julie Johnson

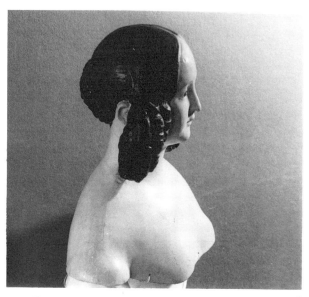

Illustration 1. An outstanding example of the 1840 period, this large papier-mâché head measures 9½" h. and remains in fine original condition. Her painted eyes have a darker and lighter ring of blue surrounding the pupil and gray finely stroked brows. Her molded hair is caught in a braided bun at the back of her head while full bunches of curls fall forward of her exposed ears. Note the full shoulders and molded breasts. *Lorna Lieberman Collection.*

Illustration 2. Reflecting the extravagance of women's hairstyles in the 1830's, she boasts endless braids and puffs. Her eyes are painted turquoise blue and her low neckline reveals a molded bosom. Her preoccupation with hair has kept her from changing her original dress of yellow silk. Quite properly she wears no drawers but has yellow silk tubes 'for show' tied on at the knees. 18" h. Milliner-type kid body, wood limbs. *Lorna Lieberman Collection.*

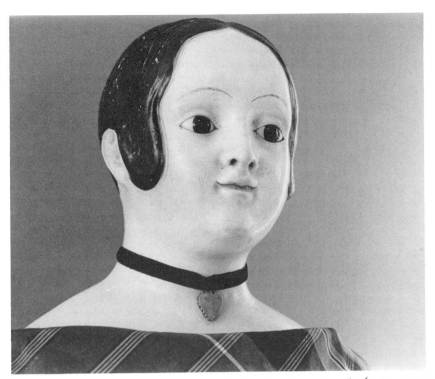

Illustration 3. 'Annabel' is full of mirth. She represents the finest in early papier-mâché dollmaking and dates from the late 1830's - 40's. Note her large milk glass eyes which are prominently set well into the eye sockets. Her molded hair is coiled into a braided bun at the back of her head. What can one say about a doll like Annabel except that she is a treasure. 31" h. French-type kid body. *Lorna Lieberman Collection.*

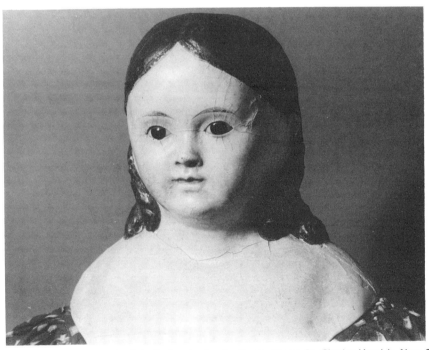

Illustration 4. 'Tillie' was owned originally by the family that built the St. Charles Hotel in New Orleans. She stands 24" tall and has 10 long molded curls falling onto her shoulders. Her pupilless dark glass eyes spell contentment. She still wears her original hand-made clothing on her plump cotton-stuffed body, the blue merino dress styled for a child of the mid-nineteenth century. *Lorna Lieberman Collection.*

These four dolls from the Collection of Lorna Lieberman

Illustration 5. She dates from the First Empire, 1800-1810, and is reminiscent of the earlier Queen-Anne type woodens. Her head and torso are of molded carton with brilliantly painted features executed with verve. Wisps of human hair poke out from her nailed-on cap of gray silk. Her arms are rolls of paper ending in four-fingered wooden fork hands. She wears her original paper underdress with elaborate gilt-trimmed gauze overdress. 17" h. *Essex Institute, Salem, Massachusetts Collection.*

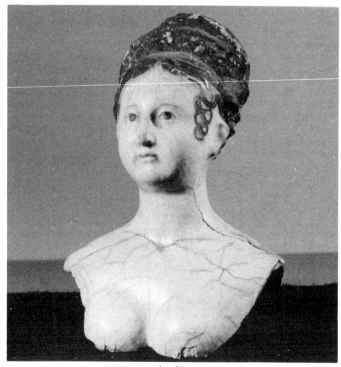

Illustration 6. A rare example of an early papier-mâché head made from laminated layers of paper and glue. Her high molded back comb is barely visible over the coronet braid encircling her head. She dates from 1815 and reflects the Grecian influence on early dollmakers. 5" h. *Wenham Museum, Wenham, Massachusetts Collection.*

A Reunion of Survivors

by Lorna Lieberman

Photography by Julie Johnson

As collectors of old dolls, we know that seldom does one come into our care revealing much of her personal past. We long to know the name of the first child who held and lover her. Perhaps most of all, we wish we could know of the protectors who kept her from harm for so many years and then passed her along to other gentle caretakers.

Two unusual early papier-mâché dolls who have come to me in outstanding original condition have shared life together (well, almost always together) for 150 years. Happily they bring with them their provenance.

Both dolls were brought to this country from Amsterdam, Holland in 1832 by Samuel W. Hawes to his niece, Mary Reed. In 1850 Mary redressed the doll (s) in apparent copy of the original clothing and in 1877 gave them to Elizabeth Hawes. It is likely that Elizabeth was Samuel Hawes' granddaughter and that she kept the dolls for the remainder of her lifetime or that in her later years passed the dolls into the caring hands of one of America's pioneer collectors, Mrs. Edmund H. Poetter of Reading, Vermont. During this ownership, they were photographed together and pictured on page 151 of Eleanor St. George's *Dolls of Three Centuries.*

After Mrs. Poetter's death, her collection was sold at public auction and the two dolls who had spent over 100 years together were separated for the first time. "Miss Mary Reed" went to live in New York and "Miss Elizabeth Hawes" came to Massachusetts to be part of a fine collection.

For many years the dolls remained apart. Then in 1976 the New York collection was sold at auction. I fell victim to Mary Reed's charms and managed to bring her home. By happy coincidence another collector attending the auction shared with me the story of the two dolls. She had learned their history from Mrs. Poetter and, in fact, her doll still retained the original hand-written note pinned to her petticoat telling of their provenance.

Two months later I received a letter suggesting that the fitness of things demanded that the two dolls be reunited and she offered to part with her doll. Of course I accepted with delight and now the two old friends stand side by side in a glass-front case surrounded by other survivors of great age and dignity.

They are apparently overjoyed to be back together again and will someday find a permanent home at the Wenham Museum, Wenham, Massachusetts.

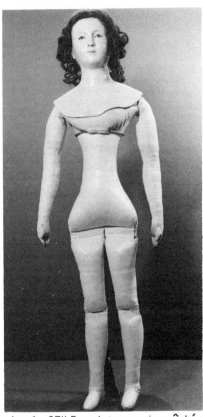

Illustration 1. 27" French-type papier mâché with rare pale blue lined and pupilled eyes set in original wax. She has straight painted upper and lower lashes and delicately feathered brows, pierced nostrils, and a pale pink mouth with darker red smile line in the center. Her original dark brown human hair wig falls in ringlets over a painted black pate well brushmarked and scalloped in the back. The shoulder plate is square cut in back but rounded in front with a molded bust. Her original body is handsewn of butter-soft white kid, the upper leg portions cut in one with the torso. The lower legs have back seaming, well-shaped calves and three-piece feet. The hips and knees are jointed by double rows of stitching 1/2" apart. Her long arms have a 2" dart giving shape to the inner elbow region. The hands are well-formed with separate fingers and set-in thumbs. Flexibility at the shoulders is achieved by a lack of stuffing in the upper arms.

47

Illustration 2. Her clothing is exquisitely hand-sewn and in remarkable condition. The two-piece white striped cotton bodice has eight tiny brass buttons and button-holes up the front and an under-bodice with six brass hook closures. Narrow scallop-edged ruffling adds detail to the neck and waist. Corded seaming extends around the neck, shoulder seam and armhole opening. Very full sleeves gather to a fitted wrist with one brass button and loop. The gathered skirt is of heavier ribbed picque with three 1/2" tucks and scalloped-edge hem. She wears long white open-work cotton stockings under her original black leather ballet-style slippers with flat grosgrain bows over the instep and narrow black grosgrain ties which crisscross around her ankles. These shoes are typical of fashionable types worn in the 1830 period and match the brown lizard shoes of her companion. Her underpinnings include split drawers to mid-calf of striped cotton with a sheer ruffle around the bottom, long cotton chemise and plain petticoat with ties. Her pink plaid coal-scuttle bonnet is of the period though its originality to the doll is in question. However, it suits her and a lady does need a new hat now and again. *Lorna Lieberman Collection.*

48

Illustration 3. 22" French-type papier-mâché with dark inset glass eyes, one-stroke brows, straight upper and lower painted lashes and pierced nostrils. The painted decoration includes a darker red line in the center of her closed lips and pink inner eye dots. She has a black painted and well-brushmarked pate with a slit to receive the human hair wig. There are two nail holes below and in back of the ears to hold the hair in place. Edges of the shoulder plate are rounded rather than the more typical square shape. The modelling of the face is that of a child. She retains her original hand-sewn cloth body with stitch-jointing at hip and knee. Her arms and hands are of molded composition to above the elbow. Although she wears old borrowed outer clothing in this photograph,* the doll retains all of her very fine hand-made original clothes, including her brown lizard ballet-style slippers with brown silk bows and crossed ribbon ties. Her split drawers are made of a medium weight ribbed cotton, (the same material as the outer dress of her companion doll), are full cut and banded below the knee with a fine scalloped edging. In addition she wears a long chemise, plain cotton petticoat and one of waffle-weave cotton with two rows of 1" tucking. *Lorna Lieberman Collection.*

*Sad to say her owner had not at the time of this photograph fully appreciated the tattered beauty of her fine original hand-made dress styled for a child in sheer red and green wool plaid with boned bodice and embroidered lace collar and cuffs. She is shown wearing this dress in the St. George book. You will be pleased to know that she wears it again, proudly . . . but backwards.

Dolls in Cases

by Ruth E. and R. C. Mathes

Primarily, the doll is a child's toy. In the course of collecting, however, we have found examples which have been diverted from their original purpose. Among these are dolls or related figures which have been enclosed in child in New England. Mrs. Imogene Anderson acquired it from a member of the family. This case was carved from a single block of wood, so that with the glass front puttied in place it was impervious to the weather.

Illustration 1.

cases so that they are not available to the child for play. We have in our collection several examples where this has occured for various reasons.

CASE 1.

In our first example this reason is the sentimental one of a memorial to a deceased child. Ill. 1 came from the gravestone of a

The doll is one of the last of the line of Maryannegeorgians, those English wooden dolls with plaster faces. We presume that the wig was made of a lock of the child's hair. The case is 10¾ inches long. A picture of this doll is shown on page 336 of The Album of American History, Colonial Period, by James Truslow Adams.

Illustration 2.

Illustration 3.

CASE 2.

The example shown in Ill. 2 was sold to us as a gravestone doll. However, it is obviously not, as the case is assembled from several pieces of wood glued together so that it would have come apart in the weather, even though the glass front is puttied in place.

There are two blond locks of hair by the head and three of darker tones by the feet, indicating the deaths of more than one child who had played with it. This is a grim reminder of the high rate of child mortality of the time. It was probably hung in the parlor as a memorial.

The doll is wax over papier-mâché with a dress style of about 1840. The blond hair is set in a cleft in the top of the head. The glass eyes are blue with black pupils. The body appears to be cloth with kid shoes and forearms. The elaborate necklace is of strings of tiny beads of many colors. The case is 14 inches long.

CASE 3.

There are no indications that the doll of Ill. 3 was a memorial doll. It may have been encased simply to preserve an heirloom. Another possibility is that it may have been considered too fragile or expensive to be played with. The dress is Empire style (which was used for children before adults). The doll has tiny black glass eyes. The cast wax head has a lightly painted indication of hair. The forearms and hands are of cast wax. The doll is surrounded by dried flowers. A label pasted on the back of the case reads; "THIS WAX DOLL WAS GIVEN IN 1779 TO MRS. DUNN OF SOUTH CERNEY IN GLOUSTERSHIRE, ENGLAND. THE GREAT-GRANDMOTHER OF MRS. KATE BAKER, NEWPORT OWNER OF THE DOLL." The case is 13½ inches tall.

Illustration 4.

Illustration 5.

CASE 4.
The doll of Ill. 4 is a wax-over papier-mâché wire-pull sleeping-eye doll with a cloth body and blue kid forearms. It is dressed in a white satin shroud. The case is shaped like a coffin and is very heavy, being coated inside and out with cement painted black. It is 14 inches long.

We were puzzled as to why the case was shaped like a coffin. Then we found an article in a folklore magazine about a custom once practiced around the North Sea. When a sailor was lost at sea, a funeral service was carried out using a surrogate figure in place of the body. Could perhaps this doll in a coffin have been used in such a ceremony for a lost child?

CASE 5.
Our next example, Ill. 5, has a colorful and festive air. Was she perhaps designed to be carried in a procession on a saint's day? This wax doll has a garland of paper flowers around the short white wooly hair on her head and more such flowers line the top back of the case. The background of brown patterned wallpaper is enlivened with a sprinkling of tiny gold flecks. The doll is tightly wrapped with no indication that she had arms nor, indeed, much of a body. Simulation of gold braid is used for edging on her frilly wrappings and for outlining a design on her chest, including a cross. This case is 13 inches long, 8 inches high and 3¼ inches deep. The glass front, top, and sides are held together by bright blue and brown passe partout.

The placing of dolls in cases is, of course, quite at odds with their original purpose; to be a toy for a child to play with. Their appearance in this form represents some special circumstance; such as, the desire to preserve an heirloom, or their use by adults as part of displays for educational or ceremonial purposes.

Diversification in Wax

Illustration 1. Wax-over-mâché head with set in hair. Wire pull at waistline to open and close pupiless glass eyes. Cloth body, leather arms, replaced clothes. *Dr. Esther G. Veno Collection. Photograph by Muldoon Studio.*

Illustration 2. 16" wax figure with wax lower arms and legs, painted eyes, human hair set into wax, cloth body, all original brocade dress and cap trimmed with pearls, sequins etc., feet bare. *Collection of the late Estelle Winthrop.*

Illustration 3. 19" Wax-over-papier-mâché doll with wire eyes, original pale blue tarlatan dress embroidered at sleeves and hem and hat with ruched blue ribbon and feather trim. *Collection of the late Estelle Winthrop.*

Illustration 4. 21" Wax-over-papier-mâché doll with molded and flocked green riding hat with feather and lace-trimmed ribbons, blonde mohair curls applied at sides with snood in back over blonde mohair pouf, apricot wool dress with matching green velvet vest. *Collection of the late Estelle Winthrop.*

Beautiful Dolls of Wax

by Zelda Hermione Cushner
Photography by Richard Merrill

Dolls of wax have intrigued me for many years and I have eagerly sought out exceptionally fine specimens. It is with great pleasure and pride that I take this opportunity to share

stockings with red striping and blue garters with blue medallions set into her boots. She wears her original two-piece brown silk gown with blue trim and brown velvet bonnet.

Illustration 1.

some of these beautiful dolls with my collector friends.

This 16 inch wax/papier-mâché lady has blue stationary glass eyes, closed mouth, remnants of her blonde mohair wig/cap which is nailed on, pierced ear effect, cloth body and composition limbs. She has molded pale yellow gloves with fine red trim and gray molded heeled boots with black and white trim. Equally unusual are her fine ribbed white

With her is pictured an 18¼ inch wax/composition young lady (right) with blue stationary glass eyes, open mouth effect with four painted molded teeth, pierced ears effect, original blonde mohair wig with braids drawn to back with ribbon, cloth body, wax/composition limbs. She has red and black heeled molded boots with gold trim. Her tattered and faded ice-blue gown has multicolor striped silk ribbon trim with old sequins and lace (Ill. 1).

Illustration 2.

The 14¼ inch poured wax doll on the left in Illustration 2 depicts a young girl with blue stationary glass eyes, closed similing mouth, brown short curled center-part human hair wig, cloth body and poured wax limbs. Her short neck is an indication of her youth as are her chubby limbs. Her blue, fine cotton dress with lace and fringe trim and tucking is original.

To her right is a most interesting early wax/papier-mâché lady, formerly of the Eleanor St. George collection. She is 14½

inches with black pupil-less stationary eyes, closed smiling mouth, auburn mohair wig, early straight limb cloth body and white kid arms from which the stuffing has gone. She wears her original cream cotton dress with lace trim and straw bonnet with lacy and floral trim. Mrs. St. George described her in *The Dolls of Yesterday* and believed her to be French in origin. She has a tag indicating that she was brought from Paris in 1838. She has a slit head into which her wig is set.

Illustration 3.

In Illustration 3 (left) is a marvelous 19 inch French poured wax lady who may represent the Empress Elizabeth of Austria. She has molded dark brown hair done in a chignon of braids in back with puffs. She has flattened brown-black wax bead eyes, closed mouth, a wood torso and upper legs and wax/composition lower legs and arms. She has black molded heeled boots and a molded chain and pendant. Her black silk taffeta gown with lace trim, embroidery, beads and sequins may be original.

Her companion is a 16-4/5 inch brown poured wax high caste Indian lady (right). She is a Montanari-type with black stationary glass eyes, closed mouth, original black center-part inset human hair wig with long braid (back), brown cloth body, poured wax limbs and original red and wine cotton sari-type costume with gold metallic ribbons, print trim, and beaded neckline. Her limbs, ears and neck are adorned with jewelry and she has a headpiece.

Illustration 4.

Illustration 5.

The 13 inch French poured wax infant on the left has blue stationary glass eyes, closed smiling mouth, blonde inset mohair wig. His head is tilted to the right. He has been redressed in white satin with gold lace trim and a halo of gilt lace. A piece of waxy ribbon with French printing accompanies this beautiful figure.

The 12¾ inch poured wax head and arms baby on the right has black sleep eyes, closed mouth, straight limb early cloth body and wears a long white cotton baby dress with tucking. Its bonnet is of pale pink with lace trim.

Amelia:
An Enchanting Beauty of Wax

by Elizabeth Anne Pierce
Photography by Richard Merrill

Graceful and serene is this lovely, gentle-looking lady of the early 1850's. Her adult features, of almost portrait quality, set her apart from her wax contemporaries. If she was intended as a portrait, who was she? Certainly she was an expensive doll for her day, and was evidently well taken care of.

Amelia is a 14'' poured wax of a delicate pinkish tint, with auburn human hair and glass eyes of bright blue. Her hair is unusually set in a center slot, like some of the mâchés and wax-overs of her period, while the eyebrows are set in, in the usual fashion. The slot is fairly well aligned with her nose, indicating care was taken in its placement. Such precision has been noted in slot heads of known German origin. Her features are well modeled on an oval shaped face. The eyes are expressive, the nose is long and well shaped, and though flattened has a well defined septum. Her lips are slightly parted, as if about to speak, and the turned pose of the head adds life to the figure. Her neck and shoulders also show a moderate amount of detail, with a hollow at the base of the throat and a faint collar bone line. In addition to this is a slightly molded bosom.

As the original clothes are still tack-stitched to the body, examination for marks and body construction is difficult, without removing them. The body is of white calico material, sawdust stuffed, with poured wax arms and legs. The arms are slender and extend to above the elbow. Her knee-length wax legs have painted-on white socks and red-brown boots with orange-red lacings. The arms and legs appear to be glued on over the ends of the cloth section arm and leg. The head is secured by cotton string sewn through the wax. The body appears to be cut in five or six sections, not counting the upper arms. The front is in two halves, seamed down the center, and includes the front of the legs. The back is cut like the front, except that it ends at the top of the seat. A separate section (or sections) form the left and right half of the seat and back leg.

The style of Amelia's clothing is markedly similar to that found on some of the smaller waxes we've seen with painted boots. The under-clothing consists of one short, one long petticoat and lace-trimmed pantalets of white calico, roughly gathered at the top and tacked to the body. The two-piece outfit is of silk

Illustration 1.

taffeta of a woven, plaid-like pattern of lavender and black on white. The jacket body is lined with white calico, and is trimmed with ruching of mauve silk ribbon. The skirt is gathered in tiny cartridge pleats on a waistband and lined with gauze. The false underbodice is of a pleated loose weave cotton, trimmed with lace at the top of two rows of the mauve ruching. The underbodice and jacket are padded out with cotton at the top for a smooth fit. The under-sleeves are of the same white cotton material as the false underbodice. Last, but not least, is her shallow-crowned, wide-brimmed hat. This is of a double layer of white net, trimmed with straw braid around the crown and edge of the brim. The underside of the brim is trimmed with a ruche of white silk ribbon, and inside the crown is a cap of white lace and sateen.

In the ten years I've owned Amelia, I have yet to come across another doll like her. It has made me wonder if she's one of a kind or one of a very few made. Perhaps, by writing about her, another one might come to light. I'd like to think that somewhere there exists a sister or sisters to this charming young lady.

Illustration 2. Fourteen inch poured wax lady in original costume.

What's in a Name?

by Z. Frances Walker

According to Winston's dictionary, the word Parian has three meanings: (1) pertaining to the island of Paros, used especially of the celebrated marble quarried there. (2) a native or inhabitant of Paros. (3) a kind of delicate, white porcelain resembling Parian marble.

Janet Johl in *More About Dolls*, 1946, said "Parian may be defined as a special kind of hard, clear paste. It was invented in 1846 by William Taylor Copeland, of England, and was termed 'Parian' because of its resemblance to the fine textured marble found on the Isle of Paros in Greece."

In the *Glossary*, the accepted term is "Parian-type dolls - - Dolls made of fine white bisque without tinting."

Parian-type is a name given to a group of dolls which are not made of marble and did not come from Paros. They are made of a very fine white clay, well pulverized which makes a very fine smooth mixture, which when dry is easily sanded to a satiny finish. Because it is so smooth it was a good medium for dainty, sharp-featured dolls. It also was possible to add to a classic head various types of decorations, flowers, feathers, ribbons and bows. As though fancy hair-dos with multiple decorations were not enough, the shoulders of the dolls were also decorated. We find collars, ties, ruffles, guimpes and beads. These decorations on both the heads and shoulders are elaborately painted.

Parian-type dolls are usually blond. There are some with light brown hair and occasionally there is a black-haired lady. We find that in some cases, the Parian dolls were poured in the same molds as china heads. It is possible to have a Parian-type head with glazed hair. The majority of Parian-type dolls seem to have blue painted eyes, but there are the exceptions with glass eyes and some have swivel necks although usually the heads are stationary.

When I first started to collect dolls, this was the most desirable type of doll to collect. They were also the most expensive. Very few Parian-type were available and when they were, they ranged from $250 to $400. This was in the days when Jumeaus sold for $75, and German characters were $35. The bisque bébés have risen in price but a really nice Parian-type can still be bought in the original price range, though the exceptionally fine and rare dolls can be double that.

Like chinas, these dolls were often purchased as heads and taken home for some member of the family or the dressmaker to construct a body and dress the doll.

After viewing some of the bodies, I cannot decide whether Mother did not know about the anatomy and proportion of the human body or whether she was not a good pattern maker. Some Parian-type heads are found on cloth bodies with bisque hands and feet. They were probably bought as complete dolls.

The fancy heads with elaborate shoulder ruffs are difficult to dress appropriately. A dress should be designed to use the decorated shoulders as part of the costume. There are many problems to be solved. Those decorations carry several different colors, making it difficult to blend the material colors with the glazed ceramic colors. These problems present a real challenge if your Parian-type doll needs a new dress.

Parian-type dolls, whether the extremely white smooth material or the lightly tinted bisque are really beautiful, stately works of art. Most of these dolls represent ladies, judging by their proportions, long graceful necks and elaborate hair-dos. However, some of the undecorated heads with curls, short necks, plump faces and shoulders, certainly have the look of children.

Parian-type dolls are a group which have been neglected by collectors in the past decade and I hope that some will again find them desirable and worthy of having a place in their collections.

Illustration 1.

Illustration 3. Parian type bisque, swivel neck, blond hair arranged high on her head, exposing the pierced ears, blue glass eyes. *Frances Walker Collection.*

Illustration 2. Parian type bisque, blond curls, painted blue eyes, exposed pierced ears, molded white yoke trimmed with molded lace ribbon and bow. *Frances Walker Collection.*

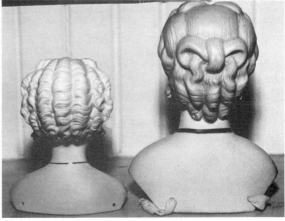

Illustrations 4 and 5. Front and back views of two tinted bisque heads with blue glass eyes, pierced ears with earrings, molded necklaces and decorations in hair. *Estelle Johnston Collection.*

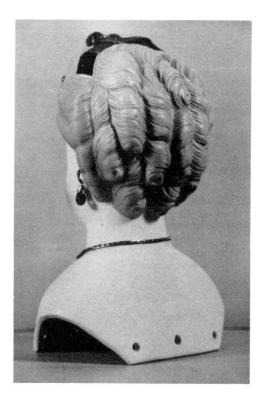

Illustrations 6 and 7. Front and rear view of parian with ornate hair style. Has molded ribbon and bow at crown of head. Note added ribbon and jewelry inserted into front of hair style, received in holes almost hidden by ornate hair style. Doll has glass eyes and pierced ears. Necklace has been added as a decoration. *Helen Jaques Archives.*

Illustration 8. Parian and parian types with a variety of hair styles and decorations including applied flowers, as well as molded combs, snoods with and without ribbon drape. Some with pierced ears. Doll second from left on lower row has glass eyes and molded guimpe with a "jewel" inserted at the neckline. *Photograph courtesy of R. A. Bourne.*

A French Doll and Her Carte De Visite

by Ruth E. Whittier
Photography by Richard Merrill

As many of you may know, people living in the 19th century had a very different way of leaving a message when making a call on a friend and the friend was not at home. A card was left which bore their picture with sometimes a message written on the back. The idea came from France and was called a carte de visite. Often the cards were left anyway and friends collected them in albums to serve as a pictorial guest book. Here is an example of the one used by Franklin Pierce, the 14th President of the United States.

Evelyn Jane Coleman in her description of the reproduction of the "Album de la Poupee," published in 1978, explains that often these cartes des visites described as "A photograph mounted on a small card, originally intended to be used as a visiting card," were kept in an album and since French dolls also used them they had their own little album with photographs of their doll friends. Back in the 1860s and 1870s, a little girl could visit one of the stores in Paris, selling French dolls and receive an "Album de la Poupee" to take home with her showing pictures of some dozen of the dolls she had seen in the shop.

Reading the information accompanying Miss Coleman's facsimile copy of an "Album de la Poupee," I realized that my own French doll, brought from Paris in 1870 by a father to his two small daughters, though not having an album, did have two examples of a carte de visite. In checking, I found that one carried almost the exact wording of the advertisement in the little album which Miss Coleman had published and was from the same shop, Au Paradis des Enfants. From Miss Coleman's translation of the page, I found that Au Paradis des Enfants is the largest toy store in Paris. It is located at 156 Rue de Rivoli and Roue de Louvre 1 and that the prices are fixed. My card does not include this latter bit of information regarding prices. My second card was from the store of Mon. Simonne, a little farther down Rue de Rivoli. These cards came to me in a small, blue trunk with a number of accessories at the death of the surviving original owner in 1944. Copies of the two French calling cards and one made of "Marguerite" in one of her original dresses are here shown.

"Marguerite" is a 16" doll with bisque head, closed mouth, painted eyes, pierced ears, white hair and bisque lower arms. Her body and upper arms are of leather. She still has three of her dresses, the one pictured of tan silk with brown silk trim, a walking dress of tan challis with blue figures and trimmed

Illustration 1. President Franklin Pierce, 14th President of the United States, native of New Hampshire. From picture of his carte de visite the original of which is at the Pierce Manse in Concord, N.H.

63

Illustration 2.

with blue ribbon and her party dress, faded and badly deteriorated. She has only one pair of French shoes, her walking shoes. Her owner had told me that she was a rather careless young lady and had lost her party shoes, her earrings and worst of all, her corsets! A kind friend did give me a replacement pair of corsets.

She wears around her neck, most of the time, a chain with a little watch suspended and when she goes walking, she has a parasol. For her other needs, the little blue trunk contains her comb, hair brush and tooth brush inside the cover. Also, there are a fan, powder box, pair of kid gloves with the tiniest of three-hole buttons on them. There is a collar and cuff set, two dainty handkerchieves, a pair of white stockings, a mirror and shoe horn. Her small fan is identical to an adult one shown

at a program on fans, in its original box from Paris, with carved ivory sticks with white silk pieces mounted on each stick.

"Marguerite" brought great enjoyment to the two little girls to whom she was brought in 1870 and when the parents had gone and the two sisters continued on in their home, she always had a place of honor on one end of the horse-hair sofa, in the parlor. As a girl growing up in the same neighborhood, I recall going in to see the owners and meeting "Marguerite" who always seemed to be a member of the family. As an adult, I attended a New Year's Eve party in the home and we were all greeted by her as one of the hostesses. Though we did not have a carte de visite with our photograph to leave, I know we all went home with pleasant memories of a delightful evening in which "Marguerite" had a part.

Illustration 3.

Illustration 4.

Illustration 5.

Illustration 6.

A. Marque
The Mystery Doll

by Rosemarye Bunting

The answers to several questions would solve the mystery of the A. Marque doll. Who is A. Marque? It would seem that he is a Frenchman from his name. Yet that is not always proof of a person's nationality today. Ease of transportation and communication not to say war or persecution has brought about a very mobile population in this world. Let us presume for the present that Monsieur Marque is French.

When and where was this doll made? On April 13, 1916, Carnegie Museum of Natural History in Pittsburgh, Pennsylvania, acquired five of these dolls from Margaine Lacroix of Paris, France. This date and her address give us the answers to when these dolls were sold and where they were marketed. The address of Mme. Lacroix was 19 Boulevard Haussman, Paris, France, at the time of this purchase by the museum. Sewn into the clothing of each doll is a woven label giving this information. Thus, we find definite answers to the questions of when (1916) and where (Paris).

By whom was this doll made? Let us suppose that it was a product of the S.F.B.J. factories. It is not only possible but probable for us to presume that this is the case as a group of S.F.B.J. dolls were ordered from Mme. Lacroix by the museum at the same time as the A. Marque dolls; together the S.F.B.J. and A. Marque dolls compose the French doll collection at Carnegie Museum . . . thirty-five of the former and five of the latter. This collection is listed as Accession No. 5581. Remember this statement is only a supposition as no facts exist among the museum's records of a proven relationship between A. Marque and S.F.B.J. except that the dolls were purchased at the same time and from the same source.

Mme. Margaine Lacroix was commissioned by the Directors of Carnegie Museum to costume a group of dolls to represent Les Reines or famous Queens of France: Marie Antoinette, Marie Leszczynska, Isabeau de Bavière, Empress Josephine, and Empress Eugenie. Madame used the A. Marque doll for this purpose. She used Models 237 and 238 of S.F.B.J. dolls to portray famous people and provincial costumes of France. A few Russian costumes and one Swiss outfit were among this section of the collection.

Illustration 1.

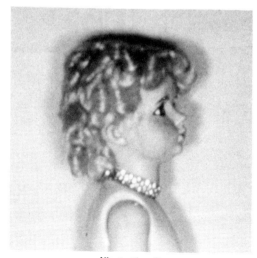

Illustration 2.

Illustration 3.

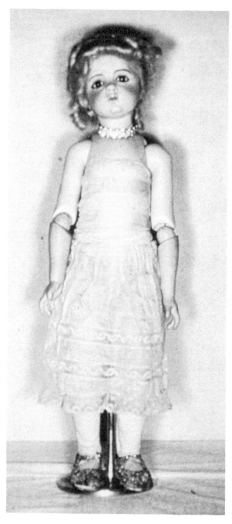

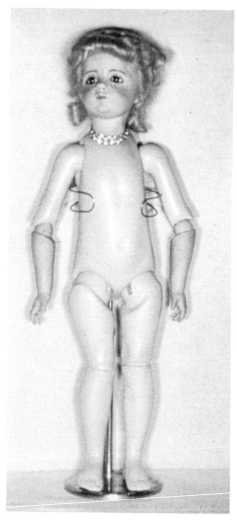

Illustration 4.

Illustration 5.

The costuming of the dolls is elaborate . . . the materials luxurious. Number 36, Queen Marie Antoinette (1755-1793) who was the wife of Louis XVI (1754-1793) of France is dressed in cream crepe trimmed with brown fur and is wearing a blue velvet coat and beret also trimmed with brown fur. The dress was replaced in 1971.

Number 37, Marie Leszczynska (1703-1768) who was the wife of Loûis XV (1715-1774) of France is dressed in gold lace with a blue velvet cloak which is lined with fur fabric imitating ermine.

Number 38, Queen Isabeau de Bavière (1371-1435) who was the wife of Charles VI (1380-1422) of France is dressed in a long surcoat of yellow and silver brocade with a tan silk cloak trimmed with brown fur and is wearing a gold and silver brocade hennin with a white veil.

Number 39, Empress Josephine (1763-1814) who was the wife of Napoleon I (1769-1821) of France is dressed in a beige crepe

empire-line dress trimmed with gold braid and red beads.

Number 40, Empress Eugenie (1826-1920) who was the wife of Napoleon III (1808-1873) of France was dressed in a three-tiered, full-skirt of beige silk with bodice embroidered with a rose motif. This dress has become a pile of dust. The wide-brimmed, light straw hat is trimmed with shocking pink and white ribbon and two bunches of artificial flowers.

At the time of accession each doll came packed in its own custom-made box, covered with beautiful French flowered wallpaper. Packed with each doll was its individual stand and label. The boxes and labels are gone while the stands are stored separately now. The stands are excellent. Each one is made of chrome steel with a looped wire to support the doll; it has a screw to permit the adjustment of the stand to the doll's height. H. Gaudermen, 69 Rue des Gravelliers 69, Paris is incised on the base.

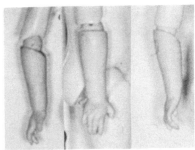

Illustration 7. Side, full front and back view of A. Marque forearm. Note how the bisque is received into the upper arm of composition.

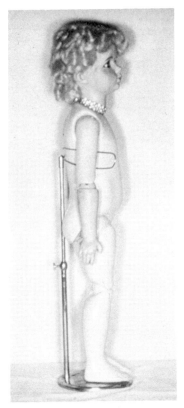

Illustration 6.

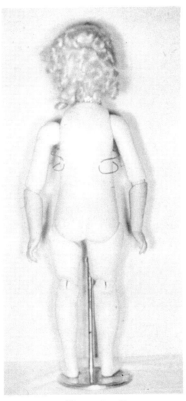

Illustration 8.

To our knowledge, there is but one size in the A. Marque doll; it is 24 inches (60.96 cm.). A Marque is incised in script at the back of the bisque head. The head is large with a high forehead, square-tipped nose, stationary blue paperweight eyes, closed mouth, square chin, protruding pierced ears, and a slender neck. Some of the wigs are natural hair and others mohair. A cardboard crown covers the open crown of the bisque head. A "pouty" look results from a slightly extended upper lip. This type is commonly referred to by collectors as a character doll. Not only the head but the forearm is made of bisque. It has straight-wrists and a ball-joint in one with the forearm. The body is composition, ball-jointed, and strung with elastic.

Each doll wears the same underwear of fine white batiste, trimmed with lace and ribbon. This is a one-piece garment made up of panty, petticoat, and camisole. In some cases there is a hoopskirt or crinoline under a very full skirt. The shoes are made the same for each doll except some are leather and others silk or brocade. The leather soles are impressed with a full-length figure of a girl, beneath which is the word DEPOSE.

In 1953 some of these dolls were selected for a display of antique dolls at Carnegie Museum. At that time they were stored in the workrooms of the Department of Man. Some years later the collection was moved to Meridian, Pennsylvania, storage facilities. Recently the collection was moved to new quarters in Pittsburgh but still the property of the Department of Man.

Again in 1971 some of the dolls were selected to be a part of the French Bisque Doll Exhibit in Hobby Hall. This exhibit was arranged under the direction of the author as one of a continuing series of doll shows. No longer are cases reserved for a doll display.

Briefly, in May 1981, five dolls from the collection were on display. One A. Marque doll and four S.F.B.J. dolls composed that exhibit. At present no dolls are on display at the museum. There was a time when the entire collection was on permanent display. Some years ago the policy was changed to one of rotating exhibits.

Nun Fashion
(Interior Body 2 Photos)

Collection of the late Estelle Winthrop

15″ Fashion-type lady doll with bisque swivel head, jointed brass upper arms and bisque lower arms, kid-over-wood torso and legs with loose kid "pants," fine old nun's habit of black wool with white linen surplice and head covering under stitched sheer black veil, black leather belt, crucifix, and rosary.

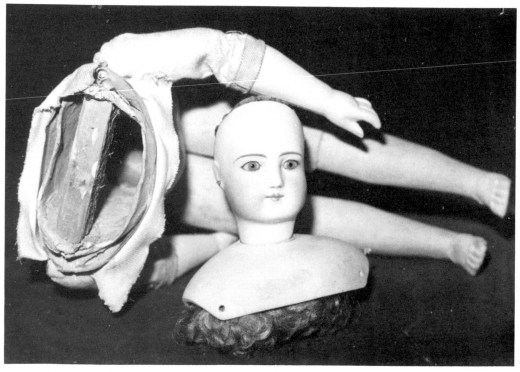

17″ Fashion-type lady doll with the twill-over-papier-mâché type body frequently described as twill over wood; here the inner construction can be seen with the wood piece attaching jointed twill-covered wood upper arms and bisque lower arms, jointed wood legs and feet also covered with twill. Although unmarked, the bisque shoulderhead bears strong resemblance to marked S&H heads.

Madeline Osborne Merrill 1907-1981
Merrill Memorial

Madeline Merrill's awareness of old dolls as being collectible originated in the mid 1940's while she was a member of a class in rug hooking. The rug hooking instructor dealt in antiques as well, and had a few old dolls on display.

Having two young daughters at the time, Madeline thought they might become interested in the type of dolls little girls of other years had played with. Her first purchase was a wax-over, squash head, with a red woolen dress, for which, she admitted much later, she had paid $30.00.

She became acquainted with other doll collectors in the eastern Massachusetts area, and was soon invited to join The Doll Collectors Of America. Madeline became a member of DCA in April of 1949. On that same day, Nellie W. Perkins of Albany, N.Y., also joined DCA. The two women became good friends, having in common a deep interest in the origin and manufacture of antique dolls, discerning taste in their acquisition of old dolls, and the mechanical and artistic skills needed for their refurbishing and restoration.

A willing participant in the activities of DCA, Madeline Merrill served with Nellie Perkins as co-editor of the 1964 and 1967 DCA Manuals. The DCA Bulletin was inaugurated in 1966 and Madeline served as its first editor. She was President of DCA from 1967-1969, and during her term in office the first three day Annual Meeting of DCA was held in Rockport, Massachusetts, to which location DCA has returned each year since.

While on a trip to England in 1968 with Nellie Perkins, with their experience gained in putting two DCA Manuals together, the idea of publishing a concise, compact book to aid novice collectors in identifying and evaluating old dolls was formed. Thus was born the first of THE HANDBOOKS OF COLLECTIBLE DOLLS in 1969, which with later additions grew to three volumes as last printed in 1977.

Over the years Madeline and her husband gave many illustrated programs on old dolls before historical societies, women's clubs, and other doll clubs. She made frequent contributions to various antique doll publications. In 1978 the Merrills wrote and illustrated the booklet entitled "THE DOLLS AND TOYS AT THE ESSEX INSTITUTE" for the Institute. At the time of her death, Madeline was Honorary Curator of dolls at The Essex Institute in Salem, Massachusetts. She wrote continually on genealogical research, and had served her term as Regent of the Boston Tea Party Chapter of the DAR.

Her own collection of dolls grew slowly yet the quality, costuming, and overall condition of her dolls remain second to none. Her first love and principal interest began and remained with the early woodens, papier-mâchés, poured waxes, good chinas, and the better bisques of pre-World War I days.

Richard Merrill

Dolls on the following pages from the collection of
Madeline O. Merrill
Photography by Richard Merrill

Illustration 1. Queen Anne.

Illustration 2. All-wood doll of Empire period.

Illustration 3. Queen Anne.

Illustration 4. Fashion Ladies.

Illustration 5. Madeline Merrill.

Illustration 7. Steiner.

Illustration 6. Breveté.

Illustration 8. China molded hair.

Illustration 9. China with dimples.

Illustration 10. Hatted wax.

Illustration 11. Glass-eyed china.

Illustration 12. Pair of Milliners.

Illustration 13. Glass-eyed papier-mâché.

Illustration 14. Wax-over.

Illustration 15. Milliner.

Illustration 16. Madeline Merrill at work.

79

Bébé Gesland, French or German? Perhaps a Little of Each

by Margaret Whitton
Associate Curator of Dolls, Margaret Woodbury Strong Museum
Rochester, New York
Dolls and flyer from the Margaret Woodbury Strong Museum
Photography by Harry Bickelhaupt

Bébé Gesland, is a fascinating example of the popular French child-like doll that captured the attention and the hearts of both children and adults in the late 1890's through the turn of the century.

The salesroom for the firm of E. Gesland was located at 5 rue Beranger in Paris from 1874-1899 and the Gesland name appears as A. Gesland from 1900 on. He died during the first World War and his widow continued the business until her death in 1924. It is thought that she perhaps concentrated on the repair of the Gesland dolls rather than the manufacture of them. Several dolls have been found with a paper label stating that the doll had been repaired by A. Gesland.

The heads for the Gesland dolls were marked FG and this is generally conceded to stand for F. Gaultier who was awarded a silver medal for his doll heads at the Paris Exposition of 1878. It is interesting to note that E. Gesland also received a bronze medal at the same time.

The body of the Bébé Gesland doll is entirely different than those of other French Bébés. Its design is constructed of a jointed, metal framework that enables the torso, arms and legs to assume different positions. This framework is padded with cotton. A flexible stockinette covering is stretched over the body giving an effect of softness even though the foundation is metal. The lower arms, legs and shoulder piece are made of a hardwood. By moving the arms, legs and waist in different directions, the doll is able to assume many positions.

Collectors have assumed that Gesland originated and manufactured this type of body, but a question has been raised in the minds of some people because of a new piece of research material that has surfaced at the Margaret Woodbury Strong Museum. A flyer was found that pictures a doll body that can assume the same positions as the Gesland body. In appearance it seems to be identical to the Gesland body except that the shoulder piece in the flyer is covered up. Printed on the bottom of the flyer is "Made in Germany." Because the flyer is not dated this information raises the question of which came first, the body supposedly made by E. Gesland or the one in Germany as advertised on the flyer, or did a German firm manufacture the body for E. Gesland? Because of this new information we can now assume that the possibility of the Bébé Gesland body having been made in Germany merits some serious thought.

We may never know the answer but it provides another challenge to collectors who are interested in researching the history of dolls and the people involved in their manufacture.

Illustration 1. FG mark on back of the head of the Bébé pictured.

Illustration 2. Bébé E. Gesland Brev SGDG 5 rue, Beranger 5 Paris is the name stamped on the back of the positioned doll.

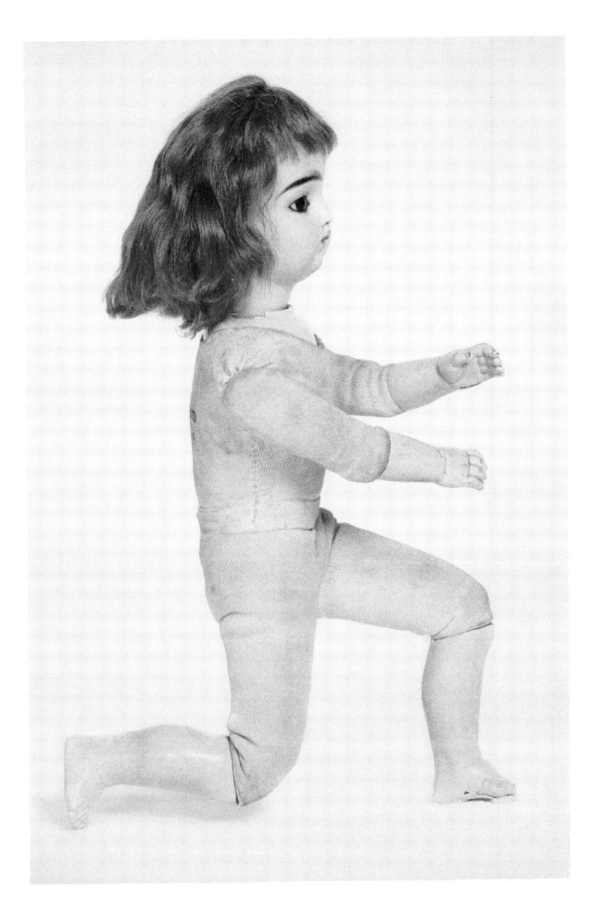

I.

1 Bein überschlagen;
beide Arme übereinandergelegt.

II.

1 Arm gestreckt, der andere
gebogen. An einer Tischkante
sitzend: 1 Bein seitwärts, das
andere gestreckt.

gesenktes Bein

III.

Knieende Stellung;
Arme gebogen.

gesenkter
Arm

IV.

Sitzende Stellung: Die Stellung ist ähn-
lich dem Sitzen spielender Kinder (auch nach
rechts möglich); 1 Arm gestreckt nach oben,
der andere nach unten gesenkt.

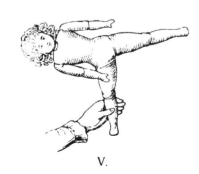

V.

Festhalten des rechten Beines und Biegung des ganzen
Oberkörpers durch einen Druck mit der Hand; man kann
auch hierbei noch linkes Bein und linken Arm nach oben
stellen, rechten Arm nach unten, mit dem Bein
parallel. Diese Bewegung ist auch nach links ausführbar.

Auslands-Patent
u. mehrere D. R. G.

„Maquette".

Neue Gliederpuppe mit völlig geräuschlosen Bewegungen.

Man beachte:

Jedes nach irgend einer Richtung bewegtes Glied, ob es wie Abb. II und III vorwärts, oder wie I und IV seitwärts bewegt wird, muss in die Stellung zurückgebracht werden, in der es **vor** der Bewegung sich befand; ers¹ dann ist eine zweite Bewegung nach einer anderen Richtung ausführbar.

(Hat man z. B. die Puppe setzen lassen und will eine Seitwärtsbewegung ausführen, so müssen die Beine erst so stehen, wie vor dem Setzen.)

Streckt man jedoch Arme und Beine nicht ganz wagerecht aus ⌐ᵂᵃᵍᵉʳᵉᶜʰᵗᴮᵉⁱⁿ, sondern senkt sie ein wenig (wie der linke Arm ⅂ an Abb. IV und das linke Bein ⟋ an Abb. III, so ist jede Vorwärts- und Seitwärtsbewegung beliebig zu machen möglich.

Jede nicht willig der Hand folgende Bewegung muss unterbleiben und ist die Anwendung von Kraft zwecklos, um eine beabsichtigte Bewegung zu erzwingen.

Ausser den abgebildeten Stellungen sind noch eine grosse Anzahl möglich. Unter Anderen: 1) Beine über's Kreuz, 2) beide Beine gespreizt wie ein Akrobat, 3) Purzelbaumstellung: Kopf gestützt, Arme gestreckt, Beine in der Luft.

Knie und Ellenbogen bewegen sich genau wie die Glieder eines menschlichen Fingers, ganz unabhängig von irgend einer früheren Stellung.

Die Glieder sind von Holz; der Kopf ist mittelst Schraubenzieher abnehmbar, daher mit einer noch nie gesehenen Leichtigkeit zu ersetzen. Das Verfahren des Aufschraubens ist patentamtlich geschützt. Schmutzig gewordene Trikotbezüge werden nachgeliefert; man wende sich dieserhalb an die Verkaufsstelle.

Patent.

𝕿he noiseless Acrobatic Doll.

Patent.

New jointed doll with noiseless movements.

Please notice:

After each movement in a certain direction whether it be forward (Fig. II & III) or sideways (Fig. I & IV), the limb must be put back into the position first held. Only then is it possible to move the same in another direction.

If the doll has been in a sitting position and it is intended to make a sideward movement of the legs, then the latter must first be placed into the position they were in previous to sitting.

If the arms are not stretched out quite horizontally (⌐), but if they are dropped a little (as shown by the left arm in Fig. IV and by the left leg in Fig. III) then every forward and sideward movement can be made.

Any movement which cannot be carried out by a slight touch of the hand should not be attempted, as the employment of force would not attain the desired purpose.

A very large number of other positions than those illustrated are posible.

Knees and elbows move exactly like those of the human body and regardless of any previous position.

MADE IN GERMANY.

Abbildungen umseitig!

Illustrations 4 and 5. Front and back of the flyer showing the positions the doll can be placed in and the directions for these positions. Note "MADE IN GERMANY" on bottom of page.

Illustration 6. Bisque head, brown glass eyes, closed mouth, pierced ears, real hair wig. The head is marked F10G. The shoulder, lower arms and legs are hard wood substance. The body is cloth covered, sewn over a metal frame and is stamped Bébé E. Gesland Brev. SGDG 5 rue Beranger 5 Paris.

Cet article n'est vendu dans aucun
MAGASIN et BAZAR de PARIS

HAUTE NOUVEAUTÉ BÉBÉ GESLAND

FABRICATION PARISIENNE

Maison fondée en 1860. — Médaille de Bronze, PARIS

AVIS. — Tous ces Bébés ont quelques centimètres de plus de hauteur.

Le plus solide des BÉBÉS par ses articulations en fer, remplaçant les caoutchoucs, le seul avec pieds, bras, buste en Bois durci, Tête biscuit, Perruque flottante; ce Bébé s'assoit et se met à genoux. S'habille avec facilité.

TARIF des BÉBÉS NUS		TARIF des Bébés habillés satin TOUTES NUANCES		TARIF Têtes en biscuits p. Bébés Haut. compris la tête. Prix.	
				25 c/m	» 60
				29 »	» 70
Hauteur.	Prix.	Hauteur.	Prix.		
32 c/m	4 50	32 c/m	9 »	32 »	» 80
35 »	5 50	35 »	10 50	35 »	1 »
38 »	6 50	38 »	12 50	38 »	1 25
42 »	8 »	42 »	14 50	42 »	1 50
47 »	9 50	47 »	17 »	47 »	1 90
52 »	11 50	52 »	21 50	52 »	2 25
57 »	13 75	57 »	26 »	57 »	2 75
62 »	16 »	62 »	31 »	62 »	3 10
67 »	19 »	67 »	37 »	67 »	3 50
73 »	22 50	73 »	43 »	73 »	4 25
78 »	26 »	78 »	50 »	78 »	5 25

L'on vend à part: Têtes, Perruques Thibet et Cheveux, Pantalons, Jupons. Souliers, Robes, Chapeaux, Plissés, Douillettes, Bonnets et Robes de Baptême, Tabliers et Corsets, Bérets, Toilettes, Bébés Maillot, Bébés Parlant, Dormeur et Nègre, Bébés Marcheur.

Vente au détail pour un Bébé
DE 0.75 A 100 FR.

PLUS DE 150 MODÈLES AU CHOIX. DE 15 c/m A 1 MÈTRE
PRIX FIXE

Illustrations 7 and 8. Paper flyer probably placed in box when the doll was sold, stating that the heads were replaceable and showing the prices for the separate heads, undressed dolls and those that were costumed. The flyer is dated 1898.

LA MAISON N'EST PAS EN BOUTIQUE

E. GESLAND, 5, rue BÉRANGER, PARIS

FABRIQUE ET MAGASIN A L'ENTRESOL
sur la Rue (Ancienne maison du Chansonnier BÉRANGER.)

1898 — DÉFIEZ-VOUS !! La Maison n'a pas changé de domicile depuis 1874.

RÉPARATION en dix minutes
des Bébés et Poupées de toutes les Fabriques
On remplace les mauvaises têtes.

Tous les jours, de 8 heures du matin à 8 heures du soir.
Fêtes et Dimanches, de 8 h. du matin à 5 h. du soir.
Du 15 Novembre au 15 Janvier, de 8 h. du matin à 8 h. du soir.
Veille de Noël et du Jour de l'An, de 8 h. du matin à 10 h. du soir.

Près du Marché du Temple et la Rue Charlot.
LE MEILLEUR MARCHÉ DE TOUT PARIS

Compagnie Générale d'imprimerie Toulouse-Paris, G. REVENCHON, agent général, 145, Faub. St-Martin. — 6140

A Touch of Genius
The French Child Doll Fashions

by Fidelia Lence
Photography by Richard Merrill

Doll collecting is a many faceted hobby containing the various aspects of other subjects that are so necessary if dolls are to reflect their owner's esteem. The most important, and also the most fascinating of these facets, is found in the study of fashion. As we collect French dolls we are given the opportunity to become more aware of the greatness that France achieved in the world of fashion. For most women, throughout the past 300 years, just the phrase "Made in France" has been the key word to all things beautiful and desirous. When one cares enough great things emerge and Louis the Fourteenth really cared enough to make France the leader in the realm of fashion and it truly became an art form. The large figures called Pandoras were one of the early methods by which the French fashions were displayed in other countries to be copied. The esteem of these fashions reflected the Frenchman's love of beauty and they became more famous than their predecessors, the Spaniard and the Italian. The importance of the French textiles cannot be over emphasized in the creation of their intricate and elegant fashions. By looking at pictures of the French Court in the era of Marie Antoinette, we can only try to use our imagination, as to the vast amount of skilled workmanship that was necessary to produce these fashions of art.

With these thoughts in mind we can readily understand why this same love of beauty in the Frenchman's heart gave us the dolls we prize so highly. Just as the French woman and child were attired by the skill of the nimble fingers of the French seamstress, so the French doll representing both lady and child was dressed just as exquisitely.

Mme. Jumeau approved about 300 new models each year, which were fashioned by the many women who worked in their homes. These models were of great interest, and were displayed at the Jumeau Shop at Rue Pastourelle. They included dresses of the French court style as well as regional and character type dresses but the majority were made to represent the fashion of that year. Fortunate indeed is the collector who possesses a French doll dressed professionally at the time the doll was made and hopefully by one of Mme. Jumeau's models. We can appreciate these precious possessions with greater enthusiasm as we realize they are the inheritance of the love, patience and skill of a past generation.

As this article concerns the French child doll dresses, the following gives a brief outline of the highlights that are embodied in the fashioning of this type of dress, beginning circa 1870.

MATERIALS:

Cotton-back satin - It is similar to modern polished cotton, but it is softer and has a silky sheen. It is a fragile material and frays and wears easily.

Velvet - (silk) It was used to some extent, especially for the larger dolls. Cut velvet was used for the coat effect.

Brocade - This was a very important material used with other materials to give the dolls a truly elegant appearance.

Flannel - This was used on a smaller proportion of dolls. It is as fine as baby flannel and very light weight. The ravages of moths leave few in good condition.

COLOR OF DRESSES:

Satin - It was usually aqua or cranberry or a combination of both, also pale blue and pink and ivory.

Velvet - Cranberry was the popular color, and occasionally the deeper colors showing the cut work of designs in it were used.

Brocade - This usually has a cream background, or pale pastels were used with very small flower designs in deeper colorings. Many just had self-designs in the material.

Flannel - The palest of aqua blue was most popular and some light pinks and cranberry shades have been noted.

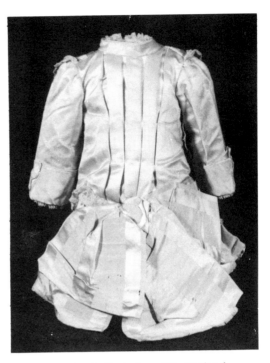

Illustration 1. Front view of dress made for 22"
Bru. Of white ivory satin, the pleats in V-shape form a
coat effect. Wide cuffs and unusual stand-up collar.
Pleating on skirt trimmed with lace and bows.

Illustration 2. Back view of Illustration 1.

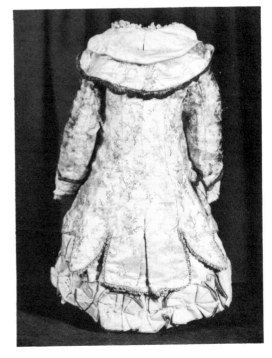

Illustration 3. Dress for a 30" Jumeau. Coat of ivory
brocade with an all-over design of flowers in pastel
colors. The plastron is ornate in ivory color, as is the
pleated skirt. There are a few vandykes at the back
and special trimming, like rosettes, used at the bottom
of skirt. The collar is double with gold lace trim.

Illustration 4. Back view of Illustration 3.

Illustration 5. Left, dress for a 24'' doll. The coat is cranberry velvet, the rest is light cranberry silk. Very ornate. Right, dress for a 12'' doll of cranberry cotton-back satin, trimmed with lace.

Illustration 6. Left, dress for a 16'' Jumeau. Aqua cotton-back satin, using pleats and gathers in plastron. Right, commercially made chemise for a 16'' Bru. Aqua silk collar trimmed with lace.

Illustration 7. Copy of a dress, made by the author, for a 10'' French doll. Aqua cotton-back satin, ivory plastron and pleated skirt covered with lace. Center, a later French taffeta coat trimmed with black velvet. Bonnet matches in black velvet. Right, a very fine white cotton dress trimmed with lace and aqua silk ribbon.

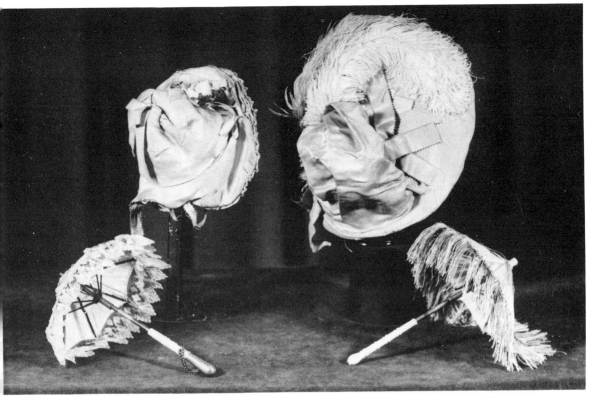

Illustration 8. Bonnets showing a pointed look to the crown and trimmed with feathers and ribbons. Two small parasols with ivory handles.

TRIMMINGS:

Hand-tied lace called thread lace or alençon machine lace was used. Frogs, small buttons (many were of the crocheted type), small silk rope, pearls, contrasting materials for piping and bias trim were used, with hooks and thread eyes for closures.

The French were not content to use just material sewn in various pleats, ruchings, gatherings, shirrings or puffings. Over this fancy work they draped thread lace, added a low waist hip belt band of piping and shoulder straps of piping.

Cuffs, collars, belts and strips of piping or bias of self-colored or contrasting color trimmed with pearls and lace and buttons were used. Collars as a rule were high neck with lace showing from underneath at the upper edge of the collar.

A pleated skirt petticoat of a tarlatan type material trimmed with lace was often sewn directly to the dress and a small amount of lace came just below the skirt. The skirt itself was pleated in either box or knife pleats or a combination of both. The coat dress jacket was used to a great degree and it was made to end at the hips or a bit longer but never as long as the dress. The portion covering the chest, called a plastron, between the coat lapels is very decorative. A plastron front example from neck down to the hip belt might have the following; fancy work starting at the neck with

fine knife pleats, followed by a section of gathering that forms soft puff effects, and then another section of pleats until the belt is reached. The plastron front usually is of a V-shape. To hasten the look of age when copying one of these plastrons, flatten the puffing with an iron.

The front view of the dress is straight and may have a tuck at the waist on the sides. The side view is flared at the back at the true waist, continuing to angle out down to the hem. The skirt is about one-third the overall length of the dress. The back can be most interesting with seams flaring outward to the low waistline and many have vandyke tabs over the main skirt with bows low at the back.

No doubt the French seamstresses had basic patterns to follow, each being individually fitted to the doll and used for the lining of the dress, but for the most part they used their own ingenuity and talents to drape here and there and obtained that certain "piece de resistance."

No French dress is complete without a matching ornate hat. The crown was often pointed with a large brim, and this was lined by pleatings and shirrings. Usually the decorations included bows, feathers and flowers.

Let us hope that these precious dresses will be well preserved for another generation to appreciate.

The Proposal

by Lorna Lieberman
Photography by Julie Johnson

A tiny embroidered linen pocket, measuring only 2½" across and just the right size for a doll, carries inside it a secret message. An envelope, complete with sealing wax on the back, announces in diminutive script *Miss A. Chamberlain Presents.* Opening the envelope reveals a wee glove cut from paper and decorated with a silver foil heart which has diamond pattern designs of woven paper.

Miss Chamberlain is answering a proposal of marriage. A proper Victorian custom, apparently for dolls as well as for young ladies of breeding, required a non-verbal reply be sent to the ardent suitor. If the lady in question returned a mitten to her admirer it would mean 'thank-you but no-thank-you.' If, on the other hand, she returned a glove it would signify acceptance.

Our poor Miss Chamberlain became so flustered by all this heady excitement that it's no wonder she lost her pocket. We hope she lived happily ever after.

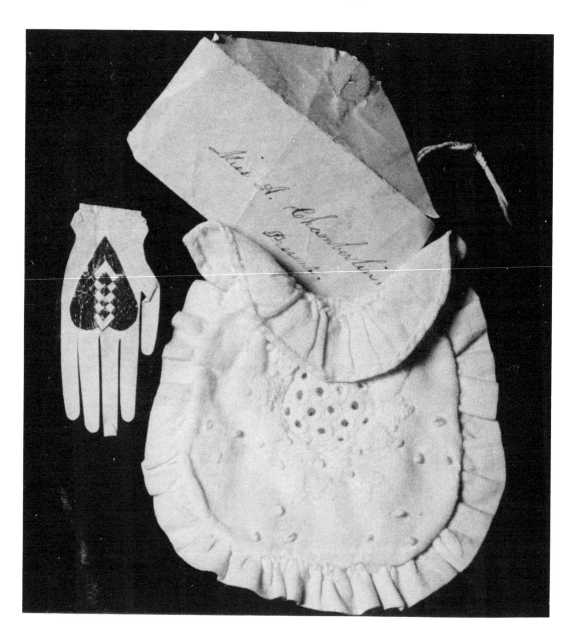

Bébé Breveté

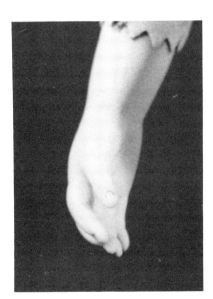

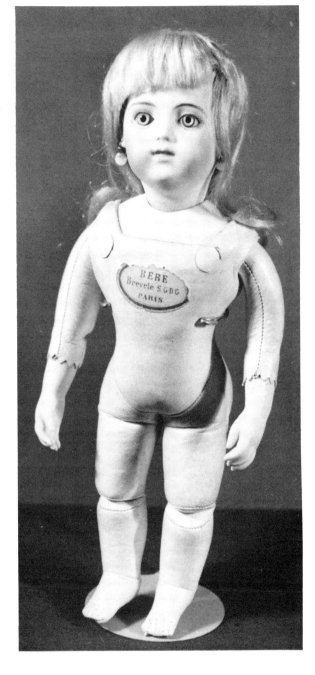

11'' Breveté SGDG; blue stationary eyes, blonde wig, pierced ears, kid body, bisque forearms, swivel head. 1/4'' down from cork pate, numerals 4/0. *Barbara Yakutis Collection. Photography by Richard Merrill.*

The Fascinating Bru

by Maurine Popp
Photography by Richard Merrill

One of the most fascinating dolls of years past is the Bru doll. Not only because of the magic of its beauty, sometimes hauntingly like one's own child, with the chubby, yet shapely toddler hands and the heavy jowled look of the very young. One ponders which Bru is more captivating, this very early one, or perhaps the one slightly later with the more delicate hands and a softer chin line of the changing, growing child. The decision does not stop at this point, for there are of course other types of Brus to consider, Bébé Teteur (a feeding doll), the sleeping doll, white dolls, black dolls, oriental dolls, all of these on the full leather body with bisque swivel head on bisque shoulder plate and bisque arms. The variation is the more slender leather body, with the wooden legs from the knees down. The feeding Bru (usually referred to as the nursing Bru), came also on a fully jointed composition body, as did the black doll. The composition body is not always marked and if it is marked, it is not always placed precisely as on the Jumeau, but can be found almost anywhere on the back torso - - proof positive the body is truly a BÉBÉ BRU. To add to the confusion, the composition body is not always just composition but sometimes a combination of composition and wood. Then again, the Bru turns up on a complete wooden child-like body. This type I have never seen marked.

In research, one does search and search and search. Oftimes becoming more confused rather than enlightened. The more I delve into the study of the Bru, the more I learn of course, and yet, the more confused I seem to be. There are missing dates. The patent papers' dates do not always agree with the Paris Directory. Some of these mysteries will be solved in time, others will forever remain a mystery. In going over the annual entries for the Bru doll it is interesting to note that the more popular dolls remained year after year, whereas the novelty dolls were fast to disappear. The one novelty item that remained popular seems to be the BÉBÉ TETEUR.

The name Bru surfaces in the 1868 Directory as "Bru Jne and Co., b.s.g.d.g. Maker of dolls of all kinds in pink or white kid, straight or jointed, crying or talking. New doll

in rubber. New doll in porcelain. New doll in hardened pate. New doll in carved wood with joints (such as those at hands and feet) giving it a graceful look. Big workshops for making of dressed dolls made always with new materials and in new styles; trousseaux. Maker of dolls' heads in bisque, rubber or hardened pate. Commission agent. Exporter. 374 Rue St. Denis." May I take note here on the word pate. It is usually translated and used as paste. However, the French dictionary has the definition as "paste, dough,//carton de." Could this mean rather than paste as so many researchers feel, that it means dolls made of carton, or to take it one step further, carton being a paper, cardboard substance, in some instances called papier-mâché when used in doll heads and often as a heavier consistency, composition. We all know there is a composition headed Bru and it would seem logical to me that this is the material mentioned, in the use of the word pate.

During the next seventeen years or so, there are many changes in the listing of Bru. I shall not go into them in detail as they have been thoroughly documented by Louella Hart in the series of articles she did for the *Antiques Journal* magazine, also in her book, *Complete French Doll Directory.* I shall however, make note of a few changes in the Paris Directories that I find interesting in regard to this article. In 1869, Bru states "movable or fixed heads in bisque, or hardened pate. Dolls' heads with two faces; crying dolls, talking dolls, two faced heads in bisque." In 1870, the most notable changes are "nude and dressed dolls, dolls in gutta-percha" [this listing follows the listing for a rubber doll]. In 1872, there are many changes, the most important being "new kinds of painted dolls in sculptured wood having in addition to ordinary joints, a jointed waist and jointed feet and hands, giving them a particularly elegant appearance." He also mentions for the first time rubber or kid dolls with arms and hands in jointed wood, also a sleeping doll with two faces (material of face is not mentioned). In 1874, he lists Musical dolls - - called magical dolls. No further changes except for an address change until 1879. Bru proudly states, "First exhibition in 1878. Silver medal." He now becomes more flowery about his work by saying, "Big maker of dolls. Specialist in new types of unbreakable dolls. Perfect workmanship. Patented doll fully jointed, in hard rubber, the only kind guaranteed as absolutely unbreakable. Dolls strikingly dressed, for export." However, an interesting addition in the listing for the '79 Directory is "Clockwork talking dolls." In 1880, the most important listing is "New discovery: Baby doll feeding from bottle (b.s.g.d.g.) in France and abroad). The new and charming baby doll in kid, feeds gently from the bottle nipple which is put into its mouth. A slight pressure on an ivory button behind the head and the baby doll functions admirably. The most pleasing toy yet made." In 1881, the additions are "Musical Baby Dolls and the Eating Doll (b.s.g.d.g.) charming surprise doll eating by itself. The firm of Bru is continually making novelties." In 1882, Bru claims 21 patents. In 1884, Bru now states 25 patents. He also lists "The Sleeping Doll, patented. This baby doll half opens then closes its eyes by the action of the eyelids."

So you see, by 1884, Bru not only made the typical Brus we are so familiar with, but he also has the feeding doll, sleeping doll and the eating doll, along with dolls in a variety of materials. By the following year they have won a medal in Melbourne in 1880. (This they make note of in the Paris Directory even though there is a time lapse of approximately four years!)

In 1881, Bru flatly makes the following statement, "The Firm of Bru is continually making novelties." What a marvelously understated sentence! No doubt the company was inventive and always striving to put something challenging on the market. The less successful types disappeared within a few years. Therefore, when one of these less saleable (at that time) dolls appears, it is a delight to see.

Years ago I had seen a Bru with a mechanism for opening and shutting the eyes, that varied from the typical sleep-eyed French bébés. The doll had always fascinated me and recently it came into my possession. How rewarding it is to be able to study her first-hand. She is the Bru Jne. with the bisque swivel neck on bisque shoulder plate, bisque arms, leather body with wooden legs from knees down. She has her full paper label across the chest. Her head is incised BRU Jne. 7, the left shoulder plate is incised BRU Jne., and the right is incised 7. Her eyes are blue paperweight and round out nicely. She does not give the flat effect of the more expected type of sleep eye. When open, they look like any other of the beautiful blown eyes. As one turns the brass knob on the back of the head, clockwise, the eyes recess into the head on a wire armature, dropping in their place, leather eyelids. Turn the knob counter-clockwise and the leather

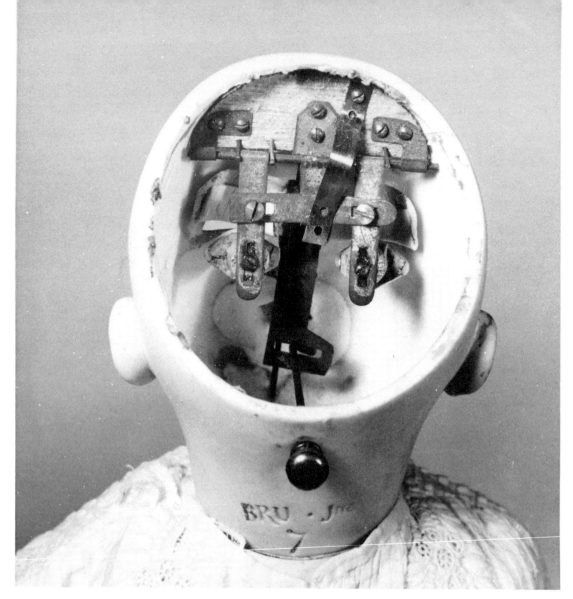

Illustration 2.

lids raise vertically inside the head and the eyes slide forward into place. Ingenious of course, practical, never! The leather lids are over a metal form and do not fit snugly as the later sleeping eyes. Due to the fact that it is two separate movements, rather than the revolvement of the eye itself causing the doll to sleep, the lid does not close all the way and because the eye itself is recessed while sleeping, there is a blank area the lid does not fill. To add to this unappealing aspect, the leather itself gives a strange cast to the sleeping face, truly a most displeasing sight. Therefore, I doubt it would delight a child, who would be interested bascially in the beauty of her doll and not the elaborate mechanism.

To add to the intrigue of this particular doll is the fact that when the eyes are open, the doll has the quality and haunting beauty of the highest caliber Bru. The features and

painting were done when Bru was still at the height of making quality dolls. She has a delicate rosy quality to her bisque, with finely brushed medium brown eyebrows, pierced ears, a dimple in her chin, closed mouth with molded tongue peeking below the upper lip. The only place a heavy hand is seen in the paint pot is in regard to the eyelashes. They are evenly stroked, yet heavier painting here and there in the strokes, giving her a rather startled expression. It would seem the paint was thickening and time was not taken to thin it.

Her clothing and wig are not original, alas! Fortunately, her shoes and socks survived. The shoes are impressed BRU Jne PARIS within an oval, on each sole.

I was sure an added advantage to this doll is that I could be sure of her age. None of that vague 1867 to 1899 all encompassing birthdate that is often so lightly stated for Brus. Having

Illustration 3.

many French patent papers in storage, I knew I had the sleeping-eyed Bru amongst them. When I uncovered the proper document, I discovered I did indeed have papers for a sleeping-eyed Bru, patent 1879, yet it is definitely not the same eye mechanism. I cannot seem to find just when this particular doll was patented. Is she the doll listed in the Paris Directory in 1884 as the "Doll with closing eyes," or in the '85 Directory listed as "The Sleeping Doll, patented"? Another mystery not yet solved. Is she earlier, or a little later, or somewhere in between? It remains to be seen. For the moment I must be satisfied, knowing she is unusual and that most likely she is the doll referred to as Bébé le Dormeur.

It would seem logical that the Bébé Gourmand was patented within this same time period. This doll was an interesting novelty because she not only feeds but would pass the food through her body and release it through the sole of her foot. Her legs are bisque and are hollow, with no sole enclosure. If the doll retains her original shoes, there is a flap on the sole that allows free access to the foot. Again, a very hard to find doll. No doubt made for a very limited time.

Also, among the papers are patents for a mechanical monkey, also, one for a mechanical goat, by Bru. Certainly not one to rest on his laurels or be satisfied with what he already had produced - - being known as an immensely successful entrepreneur. At all times the inventive mind was off and running!! It is most fortunate for us that the child of yesterday was taught to care for its possessions so well, that we in turn are free to enjoy the treasures they have passed on to us. Certainly the Bru history is an integral part of the late 1800's period of toys and dolls.

Fashion Lady

by Maurine Popp
Photography by Howard Foulke

To add to a comtemplative subject; a Bru fashion, is it marked or unmarked? Or, does it appear many different ways, as does the Bru child doll?

Having had two stationary neck Bru fashion ladies in the past, I cannot be satisfied that this is the full extent of the Bru lady doll. The stationary neck fashions were marked at the base of the shoulders - - proof positive of course. No room for questioning matching head and shoulder, as one would had they been swivel necked dolls.

Pictured here is a fashion in her original box that I believe to be a Bru. The doll is 13½ inches tall with stationary eyes that are gray blue, rimmed in darker blue, and brushed eyebrows. The pink in the cheeks encompasses the complete cheek, no rosy round dabs here. The color extends to the ear and to the chin line, to the edge of the lips and up to the outer edge of the eyes. The tiny mouth has the same coloring but two shades deeper. Her flat, rather large ears are pierced directly into her head. She wears her original blonde wig with center part and long curls. Wound through her hair is a green velvet ribbon and cluster bow that terminates in a forehead band.

The body is of leather. She has stitched toes. Her arms are articulated wood with movement at the shoulders, elbows and wrists. Her hands are slender with long separated, curved fingers and thumb.

The leather of her body is fine and firm and so secure on her shoulders that I refuse to disturb it.

The cover of her box shows a picture of two heads on pedestals and three fashion ladies. One standing behind a couch has a full leather body and wears a chemise. The reclining figure is wood articulated. It is the body structure that often comes with a head marked only with a single letter, usually deeply incised on the shoulder and on the back of the head.

The seated doll has the leather body with articulated wooden arms.

The box is gray in color with green paper binding.

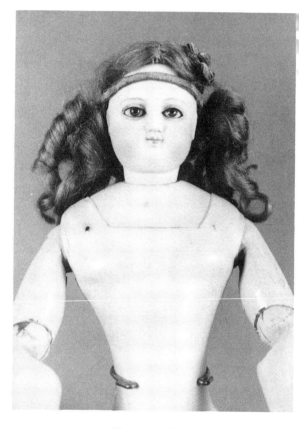

Illustration 1.

The most obvious connection between Bru and this doll and box is the fact that my Bru catalog has the box picture as part of the brochure. One of the catalog pictures also appears on a box that contains the full leather body doll with the same type head. Perhaps finally we have a connecting link with the unmarked Bru lady dolls.

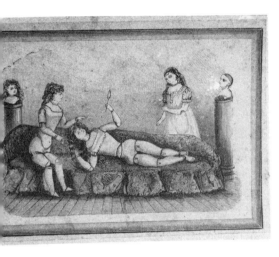

Illustration 3. Box cover for fashion doll.

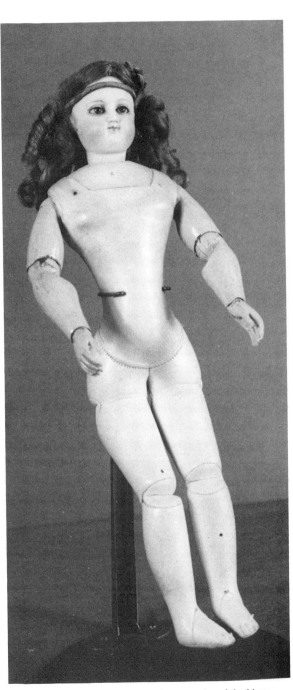

Illustration 2. 13" fashion that came in original box.

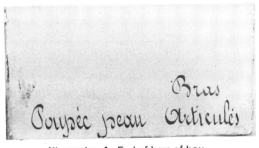

Illustration 4. End of base of box.

Black Dolls

Collection of Neil and Clara Hobey

Photography by Neil and Clara Hobey

Illustration 1. Front and side view of 8½" early molded hair papier-mâché with cloth body and wooden limbs. The head and limbs are black and the body dark brown cloth. The features are ethnic with brown painted eyes and red mouth. She has a painted necklace which was once gold. Redressed by owner.

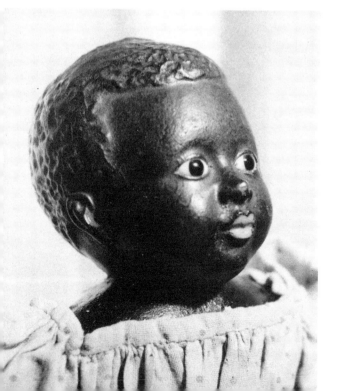

Illustration 2. 11" papier-mâché with Motschmann-type body. Cloth parts have been repaired and are brown. The body parts and head are black. The hair is molded. The ears are well done. The eyes are oval inserts of glass with dark brown pupils. Red dots in corner of eyes and nostril openings. The mouth is painted red and at the left corner of the lips is a round hole a little larger than a pin hole. Why? Her papier-mâché stomach section is well molded with navel and rolls of fat. Her lower legs and feet have folds at the ankle (not jointed), molded toes and toenails. Even the soles of her feet are well done. She is dressed in old clothes of the mid 1800's.

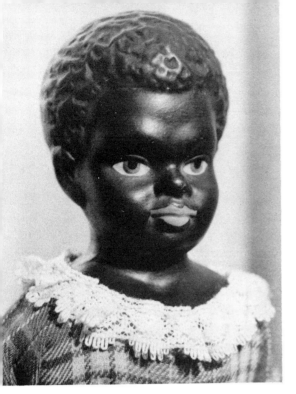

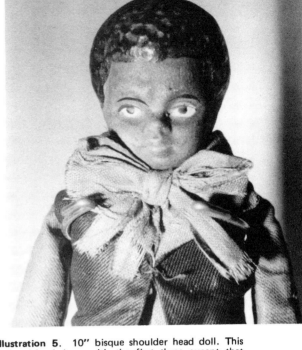

Illustration 5. 10" bisque shoulder head doll. This doll might belong with the first three except that the hair comes half-way down on the right ear and the ear is almost lost in the molding. The left ear is better. The face and limbs are brown bisque. The hair is molded and painted black. The features are ethnic. Eyebrows are defined with black painted strokes. The eyes have black pupils, lids are molded with black line at edge and red dots in corners. Nostrils are misplaced red dots and the mouth is painted red. Legs and lower arms similar in appearance to Illustration 2 and is dressed in a brown, black and orange minstrel man costume which seems to be original. The body is brown cloth. No marks or sew holes in shoulder head.

Illustration 3. 13" black bisque shoulder head, molded hair, old black cloth body, well patched, bisque arms from elbows. The lower legs are bulgy with heeled boots of painted black china. The features are very well defined, ethnic in character. The eyes have rust-red irises with black pupils. The lips are the same red but a little lighter. The ears are exposed. The clothes are not original.

Illustration 4. 16" black china shoulder head doll. Molded hair, exposed ears, ethnic features. The only color added is the whites of the eyes and the pupils are small black circles. A large number 3 is impressed on center back shoulders. The dress was made from the red and white print shirtwaist of an elderly black woman from whom the doll was purchased, by the former owner, many years ago. The body is cloth and has had many replacements over the years.

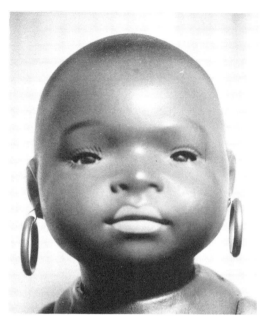

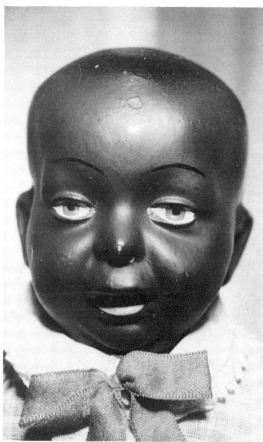

Illustrations 6 & 7. 11" black bisque baby. The body is a dark brown four joint, bent limb composition. The head is ethnic "South Sea Islander" type. It is dark brown, matching the body and is a very fine bisque. The hair is a black wash simulated baby fuzz. The eyebrows are lightly suggested and lashes both in black. Dark brown, very small sleep eyes, red painted closed mouth, pierced ears with brass colored hoop earrings complete the picture. The baby is marked Heubach-Koppelsdorf/399.11/0 Germany/DRGM.

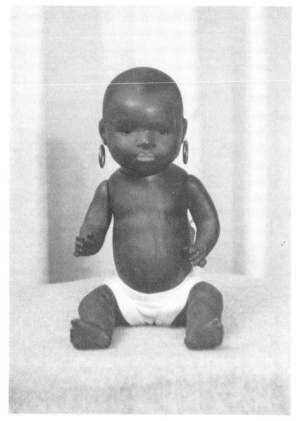

Illustration 8. 12" composition head baby doll with cloth body. Black ethnic head looks like K ★ R 100 or Baby Bumps but is marked WA9, or reversed P, on base of back neck. The head is very crudely joined to the brown cloth, excelsior-filled body with white string. The flange neck has swivel action. Metal discs have been inserted at shoulders and hips giving actions to the simply formed arms and bent legs. The arms and legs seem to be stuffed with cotton. The re-issue 1914 Marshall Field and Co., Kringle Society Dolls, Catalog, Foreword by Evelyn J. Coleman, on page 16 #C67431 shows a black doll. Bingo Junior Negro Baby in rompers; 10½"; 1/2 dozen in box. Dozen $8.00. This doll is very much like the one pictured here. The romper suit of red and white checked cotton, white collar, lace trim and a braid trim belt. No shoes or socks.

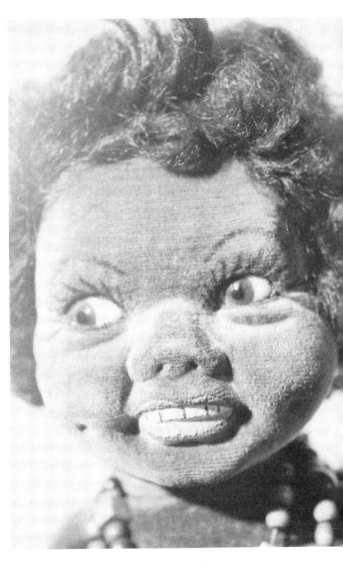

Illustration 9. 14″ brown velveteen cloth doll. The head has hard mask formed ethnic face of velveteen, inserted glass eyes with brown pupils glancing to the right. Brows and lashes are drawn in black, nostril dots of red paint and red oil painted lips with white oil paint openings marked off with black lines to simulate teeth. The head is stuffed and rows of hair are sewn on for the wig. Swivel neck disc sets on shoulders. The arms are straight with needle molded hands and are hand sewn to shoulders. The trunk of the body is to the waist only and the legs are attached here. The legs are straight with needle molded feet and toes. She wears a braided grass skirt in shades of gray to green. Wooden beads in the same shades with fuchsia added are made into two necklaces, arm and ankle bracelets and part of the earrings. White molded solid bands make the second bracelets on arms and ankles plus the upper ring of the earrings. The ears are needle molded flaps attached by insertion to the side seams of the head. They are hidden by the hair. The rings are sewn to them. The bottom of the left foot has a stitched-on black cloth label, printed in white, Made in England/ by/Norah Wellings.

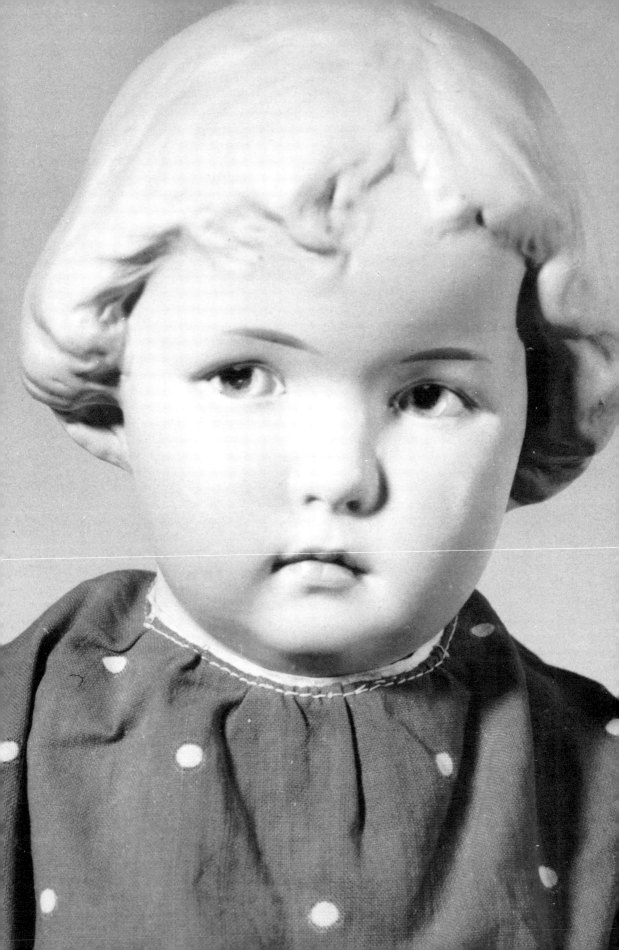

German Closed-Mouth Dolls

Collection of Dorothy P. Burton
Photography by Richard Merrill

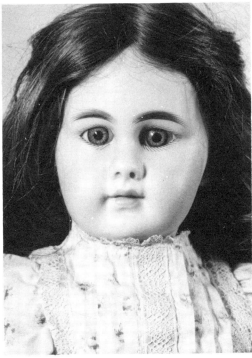

Height 15″, Mark: S 10 H
                     939
Blue paperweight, sleeping eyes, pierced ears, ball-jointed composition body with straight wrists. Replacement wig of real hair.

Height 9½″, only mark figure 3, plaster pate, ball-jointed composition body, one piece, nicely molded arms, original blonde wig.

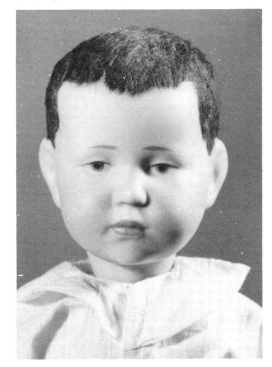

Height 12½″, Mark: K star R
                       101
Brown flocked hair, painted blue eyes, ball-jointed composition body.

Opposite Page: Height 16″, Mark: 83 Heu 58
                                      Bach
                                        3
Blonde, molded hair, blue intaglio eyes looking to the right, ball-jointed composition body.

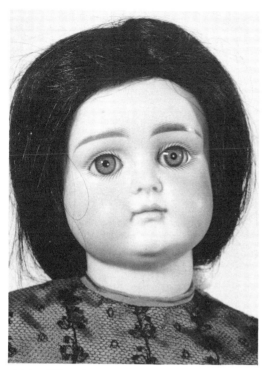

Height 15", only mark figure 10, plaster pate, ball-jointed composition body with straight wrists, blue sleep eyes. Replacement wig of hair belonging to owner's mother at age twenty-four.

Height 20", Mark: Made in
Germany
128
Brown sleep eyes, original blonde wig, ball-jointed composition body.

Height 24", only mark numeral 15, brown sleep-eyes, ball-jointed composition body with straight wrists, dark blonde original wig.

Height 25", Mark: 870 H 12, solid dome, dark brown real hair wig, stationary brown eyes, pierced ears, deep molded shoulder plate, cloth body, kid arms.

Height 16½", unmarked, solid dome, stationary, blue paperweight eyes, head turned to the right, nicely molded, deep shoulder plate, kid body, bisque hands and arms to elbow, original flaxen blonde wig.

Height 14", unmarked, solid dome. Definite downward tip to head position, stationary, paperweight blue eyes, nicely molded, deep shoulder plate, kid body with bisque arms to elbow, original blonde wig.

Two Unusual Simon Halbigs

Collection of Dorothy McGonagle
Photography by Richard Merrill

1049
S 4 H
Germany

12 inches tall, this wide-eyed Simon Halbig has two large square teeth and bears a resemblance to the earlier 949. Her body is fully jointed, including wrists, and is of excellent quality. Her bisque is also excellent, with a lovely sheen. Her eyes are almond shaped, unlike the 900 series Simon Halbigs, which tend to have close-set eyes. This 1049 may be a transitional doll between the 900 series and the very popular 1079. She probably dates from the late 1890's.

1339

S & H
L L & S
8

19 inches tall, this unusual child, dressed as a schoolboy, is in the 1300 series, which includes the 1329 Oriental and the 1358 Mulatto. This sweet-faced child has very subtle characteristcs of both. He has a somewhat flat nose, his mouth is close under his nose and also flatter, which gives the appearance of a modified "undershot jaw." It is a subtle thing, but gives a very human look (semi-Oriental, yet the coloring is beautifully Caucasian). The L.L.& S. is possibly Louis Lindner & Sons (see Coleman's Encyclopedia p. 390). This S.H. 1339 may be a "character" made exclusively for them. The body is not of Simon Halbig quality; I would question its originality, but for the dual company involvement. He probably dates from about 1910.

Twin Dolls

Twin dolls with matching trunks. Mark: 143. Height: Nine and one quarter inches. Sleeping eyes, one with brown eyes, the other with blue eyes, open mouth. Trunks contain dresses, shoes, hats and underwear. *Mary Kiley Collection. Photograph by Richard Merrill.*

Cloth Dolls

by Pearl Morley
Photography by Richard Merrill

Izannah Walker: 17" doll made in Central Falls, R.I. during the last half of the 19th century. Dress copied from original.

Enigma or Mystery doll: These dolls appear to date from 1849 to 1860. This 25" doll is unmarked and has stiff wire rimming the shoulders to hold the shape.

Chase dolls: These dolls were made in Pawtucket, R.I. starting in 1891 by Martha Jenks Chase. (a.) 17" doll believed to be early unmarked Chase (left). (b.) 26" Mammy. Paper label reads "The Chase Stockinet Doll/made of Stockinet and Cloth" (right).

Alabama dolls: Made by Ella Smith of Roanoke, Ala. (a.) 17" doll marked on body "Mrs. S.S.Smith/Manufacturer/Roanoke, Ala."; marked on lower torso "No.1/Patented Dec. 1907"; blue shoes (left). (b.) 19" black Alabama marked on body "Patented Sept. 26, 1905/No 1"; marked on leg "Mrs. SS Smith/Manufacturer of and Dealer in The Alabama Indestructible Doll/Roanoke, Ala."; red shoes. Believed to be in original red dress.

Sheppard doll or Philadelphia baby: Made by J. B. Sheppard & Co. of Philadelphia, Pa. around 1900 to 1935. (a.) 21" doll with pouty expression and blue eyes (left) (b.) 22" doll with brown eyes (right).

Columbia doll: These dolls were made by Emma E. and Marietta Adams, Oswego, N.Y. in the 1890's. This 15½" doll is unmarked.

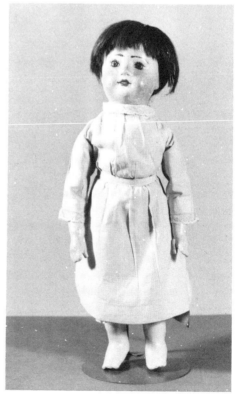

The doll on the left is a mission doll originated by Mrs. Julia Jones Beecher of Elmira, N. Y. Dolls were made by the sewing circle of the church from 1893 to 1910. Note the detail of the dimpled fingers. (a.) 21" white baby (left). (b.) 19" black adult figure. There are many similarities to the Beecher (note the mitten hands). It has not yet been established that it was made by the same group.

Rollinson doll: Designed by Gertrude F. Rollinson, manufactured by Utley Doll Co., Holyoke, Mass. from 1917 to 1919. This 18½" doll is unmarked but has painted-in teeth and a wig. Some of these dolls were fashioned with painted hair.

Presbyterian dolls: These dolls were first made in 1885 to raise money to build the First Presbyterian Church, Bucyrus, Ohio. The dolls were made again in 1956 and can still be purchased. (a.) 16½" doll purchased March 1973 (left). (b.) 17½" early doll with original clothes (right).

Primitive or folk art cloth dolls: Many were made in the mid- or late 19th century. (a.) 26½" early home-made doll, probably in original clothes (left). (b.) 23" early homemade doll (right rear). (c.) 16½" early homemade doll (right front).

The Men in my Life

by Eugenia Shorrock
Photography by Richard Merrill

No. 1.   No. 2.   No. 3.   No. 4.   No. 5.

I know 'tis said that it's not the men in your life that count but the life in your men. Since the breath of life is not in them, as all will agree, it would seem that they must not count for much. However, quite the reverse is true. I cherish them highly!

In the Kammer and Reinhardt catalogue, published in 1927, entitled, "My Darling Dolls," they are described as follows; "Highly original character dolls. Light as a feather, wire frame, felt cloth clothes, cloth faces. Height about 33cm., weight 80 grammes; with character heads of most durable material, fine drill varnished and well painted, moveable by means of wires in arms and legs."

Dolls representing all professions and trades and soldiers of other nations were offered, "if colored illustrations are sent in." Each of the men is highly characteristic of the profession or trade he represents.

The first gentleman in the photograph, No. 1, is the *Reverend,* the only one of the ten without a hat. He is dressed in checkered pants, white spats, white shirt and collar. His costume is topped off with a black, cut-away coat and green tie. His ruddy face, accented by a monocle in his right eye, is framed with white side-burns. He wears a worried look as he ponders whether his message to his congregation will have the desired affect.

No. 2, the *Lawyer,* is dressed in a gray felt suit and black tie, white spats over black shoes and topped off with a large, gray, broad-brimmed hat. He, too, wears a monocle in his right eye as he smokes a large cigar. His confident, swaggering air leaves no doubt that he has a record of winning his court cases.

No. 3, the *Sailor,* wears patched, bell bottom pants, double breasted pea jacket with a brown and white checkered scarf inside the collar which is set off with a gold button, and a beret type sailor cap, adorned with a gold button on the front. The sailor is raising his right hand toward his mouth, behind which he confides, no doubt, some juicy piece of gossip to his neighbor, the salesman, who is our next character in the line-up.

No. 4 is the *Salesman,* or drummer, with a three-quarter length, flowing gray overcoat. He wears a black and white checkered, visored cap, out of which appear fuzzy sideburns. He munches on a big cigar and has a portfolio of his wares under his arm. His pants are a darker gray than the overcoat. On his face is a bored expression as he listens to the sailor's information.

The No. 5 gentleman has all the ear-marks of a *Dude.* He is dressed, to the minute, in a chic brown three-quarter length coat with wide cuffs on the sleeves and a black velvet collar and two matching buttons. He wears black pants, white shirt with a white silk bow tie. On his confident head he wears a tall silk hat. He also wears a monocle in his right eye and carries a cane in his white gloved hands. His hair is as white as his eyebrows. His left eye is closed, as he peers upward through his monocled right eye at something skyward, which has caught his attention momentarily. White spats over black shoes contribute to his air of confidence.

No. 6.   No. 7.   No. 8.   No. 9.   No. 10.

No. 6, in photograph 2, may be my favorite of the ten, our *Hobo.* His unconcerned, alert expression, his upstanding eyebrows which suggest horns, his huge nose and unshaven face with the large "stogie" in his mouth, and his ruddy cheeks, when taken all together make a countenance that no one could love but me, but you know, they say there is no accounting for tastes! He wears a badly abused, gray felt hat with a black band around the crushed crown. A tan, burlap-jersey top under a shrugged-back black jacket over sloppy, gray pants contributes to his appearance. The fact that his fly gaps dangerously, concerns him not at all! Around the neck of our "hero" is a jaunty, bright red scarf, with the ends flying wide. His huge bare feet are bony and bunioned, ample for the life of a wanderer. On the bottom of one foot is stamped the word, Germany.

No. 7 is the *Apache Dancer.* He wears a checkered bicycle cap with a visor, a red jersey, gray pants and a navy scarf wrapped around his neck. His hands are in his pants pockets. His hair, with sideburns, surrounds a very sour-puss expression.

No. 8, the *Professor,* absented-minded as they are reported to be, has not forgotten his green portfolio. He is an elderly gentleman with white fur beard and sideburns, ruddy cheeks and spectacles. He wears gray felt pants, black shoes and a three-quarter length black coat. A white shirt and black bow tie complete his costume.

No. 9, the *Bell-Hop,* is resplendent in a bright red uniform, a jacket trimmed with gold braid and ten gold buttons. He wears black shoes and his ruddy cheeks match the red of his uniform.

No. 10, the *Bus Announcer,* is dressed in black pants and jacket over a white shirt and black tie. He wears a long, dark green apron over all and atop his head is a visored cap with a gold band around the crown. A large watch chain leading to his left pocket, indicates his occupation, watching the arrival and departures of buses.

Where from and whence did I obtain my treasures? When I was in the Sportsmen's Shows with my reptile exhibit, in the late 1920s, I was taken to the laboratories of a theatre lighting-effects expert and there on a shelf, these dolls were arranged. If I was told where the dolls came from, I do not remember. It was not important, at the time, as I was not yet a doll collector.

Many years later, in 1971, my close friend decided that the dolls would mean more to me than they did to her and presto, I became their new owner!

Lenci Dolls

A lovely example of Musette, the Lenci lady doll, created in 1925/26. Twenty-nine and a half inches tall, she has the typical, half-shut, dreamy eyes. The plumed bonnet matches her gown of French blue felt. The full skirt has narrow cross-bars of magenta felt and the low neckline is trimmed with a ruffle of magenta. Over her leg-o-mutton sleeves, she wears a dainty, silk-embroidered and yarn-fringed shawl of white cashmere. Under her skirt is a ruffled organdy petticoat and a hoop skirt. A pretty pair of garters, fashioned of felt roses, serve the dual purpose of keeping her silk stockings up and keeping down the ruffles of her organdy pantalets. Pointed tipped, high-heeled patent leather slippers complete her costume. *Helen V. Patry Collection. Photograph by Richard Merrill.*

The Lenci doll on the left is known as Lobelia Boy. Fourteen inches tall, with dark blonde hair and brown eyes turned to the left, he wears a white cotton shirt, green felt jacket with orange trimming and two brass buttons. His trousers and shoes are of brown felt. His socks, knitted of beige wool, are trimmed at the top with a brown design. In his left hand he carries three dark blue lobelia blossoms and on his right arm is a wicker basket of the same flowers. Lora (or possibly Sora) on the right of photograph No. 2 is fourteen inches tall and dressed as a Corsican maiden. Her hair is black and her eyes painted brown. Her blouse is white cotton with deep cuffs of black felt, edged with yellow. The bodice is black felt, edged and tied on the shoulders with orange felt to match her headdress which is trimmed with narrow white lace and yellow felt. Her full skirt is of green felt, trimmed with inch wide bands of yellow and orange and a long, orange felt apron trimmed with two inch wide bands of white with appliqued and embroidered trimming. Both dolls have a label;   Bambola Italia
Lenci
Torino   and
Made in Italy

Cloth label - Ars Lenci
        Made in Italy
        Torino, New York
        Paris, London
Helen V. Patry Collection. Photograph by Richard Merrill.

Steiff Mechanical

Ten inch tall mechanical Steiff dressed as a London bobby. He has a key-wound spring mechanism that advances his feet that are on rollers, in a walking motion. There are checks on the mechanism that allow the legs to move forward only but he moves in a circle. There is a stop/start lever on his back. His face is made of felt with a seam down the middle, black button eyes and applied felt ears. His arms are jointed at the shoulders and his cloth hands have stitched finger separations. His suit is navy blue felt with gold buttons and belt. There is no button in his ear but early Steiffs did not have the button. *Bonnie Jeannette Collection. Photograph by Richard Merrill.*

W.P.A. Dolls and Puppets

by Elizabeth MacMahon Donoghue
Curator of Dolls, Wenham Museum, Wenham, Massachusetts
Photography by Richard Merrill

In August 1980, a visitor at Wenham Museum from Leavenworth, Kansas, told of 96 sets of W. P. A. dolls in St. Mary's College Library in Leavenworth. She inquired if we had any. We didn't.

We learned that Doll Collectors of America members Zelda Cushner and Pearl Morley had acquired choice W. P. A. dolls and puppets.

A few days later, a Wenham Museum volunteer brought in an advertisement from the Antique Trader Weekly, Dubuque, Iowa, of August 15, 1980, offering "rare W. P. A. dolls, an Irish pair."

For one who, over the years, has given many programs and exhibits on Irish Dolls and Treasures, the words "an Irish pair" were irresistible. A telephone call to Colorado made them mine.

On September 4, the welcome Irish pair arrived and were given to Wenham Museum. It is a proud boast that Wenham Museum has never bought a doll. All are gifts of friends.

Two days later, at a Doll Collectors of America meeting on Summer Finds, among the dolls displayed were those pictured here. It was the first time most of the members present had seen W. P. A. dolls.

The Works Progress Administration (W. P. A.) was started in the depression of 1933 in Franklin Roosevelt's presidency, to relieve unemployment. One of the many effective projects of the New Deal was figurine and dollmaking, under the direction of artists. The workers earned about $20 a week.

The faces of the dolls were made of a variety of materials, including cloth, composition, hard rubber, plaster, and silk-screened cloth. Bodies were constructed of cloth, composition, or wood. Most dolls were 12 to 14 inches and others 22 inches tall. Some figures showed regional costumes of the 1600s to 1900s. Others portrayed historical persons. Many were made in boy and girl sets on wooden platforms.

These creations were welcome visual aids in schools, colleges, and libraries, as well as affording much-needed employment to the workers. They are truly benefit dolls. Most of the dolls were made in Emporia and Wichita, Kansas and some in the Birmingham, Alabama area. They were given or sold for $1 to schools country-wide.

Ruth Whittier recalls W. P. A. workers in the State Library of Concord, New Hampshire, mending books and making puppets. Puppet shows were put on in libraries and hospitals.

Now, almost a half-century later, these dolls of the early 1930s are eagerly sought. Inflation of the 1980s has increased the price. The colorful and well-made W. P. A. dolls, charming bits of Americana, are desirable additions to any collection.

Sources consulted:

Flack, Thelma C., "The Dolls Collectors Forgot, W. P. A. Dolls," *The Antique Trader,* 40, 41; Feb. 25, 1975.

—— "Something Old-Something New," *United Federation of Doll Clubs Region 4 Souvenir Book,* 34, 35; 1978.

Haight, Eleanor, "Milwaukee Women Sponsor W. P. A. Doll," *U. F. D. C. Milwaukee Convention Book,* 15, 16, 17; 1975.

Kepner, Richard, "Delightful W. P. A. Dolls," *U. F. D. C. Region 4 Souvenir Book,* 11; 1975.

Kimport, "Work Ethic," *Doll Talk,* 1, 2; Mar.-Apr. 1981.

Whorton, Judith, "Ambassadors of State," *U. F. D. C. Region 9 Souvenir Book,* 54, 55; 1977.

—— "W. P. A. Dolls and Puppets," *U. F. D. C. Region 9 Souvenir Book,* 43, 46, 47, 48; 1979.

——"The U. S. Government made W. P. A. Dolls," *Spinning Wheel,* 26, 27; May, 1973.

——"The U. S. Government made W. P. A. Puppets," *Spinning Wheel,* 50, 51; Nov. 1973.

Scarlett O'Hara Mammy Doll 14''. Believed to be a W.P.A. doll - made in Macon, Georgia about 1937. Painted face, yarn hair, black and white print dress with white apron, full petticoat and pantalettes. Black, high laced boots made from typewriter cover material. She carries a white baby with painted face. Seems to be unmarked. *Pearl D. Morley Collection.*

Pearl D. Morley Collection.

Irish Couple - - heads of composition with cloth bodies. Credited to *Kansas W.P.A. Wenham Museum Collection.*

118

Pair on the left from the *Collection of Pearl D. Morley.* Pair on the right from the *Collection of Zelda H. Cushner.*

From the *Collection of Zelda H. Cushner.*

London's Oldest Toy Shop

by Mary Hillier

The dapper little Japanese gentleman stopped me, bowed slightly, and asked politely "Ham-rees?" When I smiled and looked puzzled, he added "toys, please?" The Japanese have difficulty in enunciating the letter "L" so I suddenly realized he was in fact looking for Hamley's shop. Since I was walking along Regent Street carrying a large replica of Paddington Bear which I had just bought, I was an obvious target for his query.

Hamley's famous toy shop is now at 200 Regent Street, London. It is a regular wonderland for children, with five floors of toys and dolls to explore including all the present day electronic games and mechanicals. Understandably, the shop is a Mecca for the visiting tourist seeking souvenir gifts.

In 1960 Hamley's celebrated its bi-centenary. The original little shop called "The Noah's Ark" was founded in High Holborn in 1760 by a Cornishman, William Hamley. An early engraving shows ladies in crinolines looking in a shop window where toy animals progress two by two as in the Ark story. Already an agent for European toy makers, a range of tin soldiers and wooden dolls was stocked. After this original shop burnt down in the early 19th century Hamley's was re-established at 86 High Holborn and listed as the "European Toy Warehouse." Besides the import trade, toys were exported to India and the colonies and to America as the business expanded. W. H. Hamley, grandson of the founder was born in 1843. He built up the store for over fifty years, specializing in conjuring tricks as well as selling toys. He was an agent for the popular "magicians" who performed at Victorian children's parties. During his ownership the shop also acted as agent for the famous firm of Pierotti who made fine quality wax dolls. The family worked from their home in South West London. Hamley's exhibited their renowned dolls and also advertised their repair service.

When Table Tennis became popular at the end of the century, Hamley's promoted the game under the name of Ping-Pong and scored a big success with their boxed sets. When W. H. Hamley died in 1916 his five sons inherited the business. The eldest, John Green Hamley, seems to have made a speciality of the wartime output of some British firms who attempted to supply toys in place of the German trade made obsolete by the War (1914-18). He patented a number of interesting and popular dolls and mascots, some of them made of fabric, such as Dean's and others with the newly established products of the Staffordshire potters. Examples of those patented under the Hamley trademark were:

Buster Brown, Patent No. 265,091, 22nd July 1904 (after the comic strip character invented by Richard Felton Outcault in the New York Herald) A child with flaxen hair, tunic suit, patent shoes and a little dog.

Ni-Ni, No. 334, 072, 1st June 1911

Elfie, No. 357,975, 20th January 1914

Pooksie, The War Baby, No. 358,234, 30th January 1914 A caricature baby doll made of china by Wiltshaw & Robinson Ltd., Staffordshire, in three sizes. The doll was designed by Mabel Lucie Attwell*, the famous children's book illustrator. Naked, save for soldier's cap and belt, the doll had moving arms, goo-goo eyes and a heart on its chest with trademark name.

Fumsup, No. 359,090, 25th February 1914. Also based on an Attwell design.

Lulu, The Red Cross Nurse, No. 374,013, 31st July 1916

Wu-Wu, The V.C. doll, No. 374,014, 31st July 1916

Blue-Stocking dolls, No. 379,471, 22nd August 1917

All of these dolls are comparatively rare and were probably not produced in very large numbers so it would be interesting if any occur in American collections. The doll pictured here is Wu-Wu the V.C.** doll. Made of mat-finished pottery (feldspar, like many products of the English potteries). This figure stands 6½ inches high and is clad in a skimpy white vest decorated at the back with a green heart-shaped label with name and No. of patent. On the front there is a golden V.C. on a red bar. He is prettily painted with blue eyes, rosy cheeks, dimpled pink knees and blue socks. Like Fumsup, the dolls Lulu and Wu-Wu were no doubt also designed by Mabel Lucie Attwell and typical of her stocky, chubby children. "Thumbs Up" was a hopeful slogan used in the 1914-18 war, just as in the second war the

Churchillian Victory V sign was indicated with raised fingers. The dolls were made at Hancock's Pottery, Staffordshire, one of the largest producers of doll heads at this time.

The final doll in the list, the Blue-Stocking doll, was made by a firm called Harwin at the Eagle Works, Finsbury Park, London. Their star designer was the daughter of the owner, Dorothy Harwin, and she produced Dot's Dolls and Dot's Animals on fancy fabric. The Blue-Stocking Kid was a soft stuffed doll dressed in linen hat, dress and petticoat. On each was printed different rhymes of an educational nature, presumably to help the little owner grow up to be a "blue-stocking" or academic. (In 18th century England, a society of women was formed who wished to study serious matters and wore blue stockings in place of black to proclaim their membership.) Harwin also produced Teddy Bears and two of their mascots, Gay Dog and Lucky Jim were the first mascots to fly the Atlantic Ocean. They were carried by Alcock and Brown on the flight of June 14, 1919 from Newfoundland to Ireland.

The 1915 Harwin line included Tipperary Tommy, Kittie, Sailor, French Soldier, Scout and Dixy Kid character dolls, and in 1916, Pyjama Baby, Red Riding Hood, Wee Willie Winkie. In 1917 they also produced Eyes Right Mascot dolls with Hancock pottery heads. By 1919 the wartime titles were less noticeably in the list, Peggy Pimples, Pank (reference to Mrs. Pankhurst of suffragette fame), Tinkles, Wobbler, Bo-peep, Snow Boy, Dutch Girl, Minnie Ha Ha, Rosebud, Zulu Chief, Zazz and Father Christmas.

Patriotically motivated, Hamley's stocked increasing numbers of British toys and dolls. Many firms had become well established because of lack of foreign competition. However, the depression period of the 1920s led to a sad recession in the toy trade and by 1931 the firm was forced to go into voluntary liquidation. The family shares were bought by the famous firm of Walter Lines (Triang metal toys and wooden doll houses). The name was retained and the shop was run by Walter Lines and later by his daughter, Peggy Lines, until her retirement in 1971. Now the shop, run by the Debenham group, is as popular as ever and more international than ever in its 200 years. It would be nice to know of any early dolls in American collections which bear the Hamley stamp or trademark and the author would be glad to know of any examples.

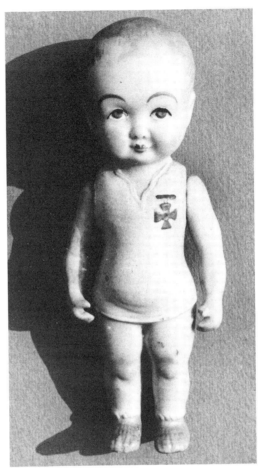

"Wu-Wu" the V.C. doll. *Mary Hillier Collection. Author's photograph printed by Richard Merrill.*

*Mabel Lucie Attwell was a London artist born in 1879 who enjoyed a great vogue with her cheerful and stylized drawings of children. During War I many of them appeared with joke captions on postcards sent by soldiers to their wives. Her designs are still popular but the dolls made to her pattern are rather rare and sought after.

**V.C., the Victoria Cross is the most famous British decoration for valour and was founded by Queen Victoria in 1856. Given for deeds of conspicuous bravery, it was a simple bronze maltese cross on a ribbon, red for the Army and blue for the Navy. It carried a small pension and enormous prestige as it was awarded very sparingly. Whatever letters a person may have after his name, the V.C. has precedence and the treasured medals fetch a very high price if they are ever sold. Normally, of course, they are retained by a hero's family.

"FINKS I'LL HAVE IT WAVED

A helping hand.

Postcard Collection of Mary Hillier. Photographs by Richard Merrill.

Schoenhut Girl in Her Original Box

by Maurine Popp
Collection of Maurine Popp
Photography by Howard Foulke

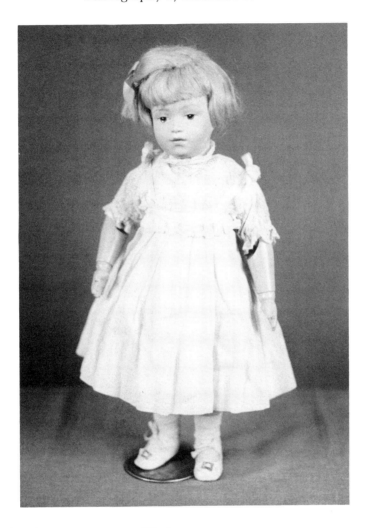

The Schoenhut box cover states, "Real Character Faces as you see Pretty Children every day on the street." The box is home to a doll that fits the cover description perfectly.

With her blue carved eyes and soft blonde wig and warm little smile, she certainly could be one of the pretty children one sees every day on the street. She is 14" tall and wears original underwear. The dress is right and proper for the period but I cannot promise it is an original. Her socks and shoes have the holes to receive the stand, in the proper manner. The doll is sweet, demure and very huggable, as you can see from the photographs.

The construction of the box is almost as interesting as the Schoenhut construction

itself. The photograph shows the box bottom opened flat. You can see where the doll was tied in place. Also note the faint creases at the corners, showing how the sides fold up into place. There is very little wasted space on the box. The sides are covered with pictures of Schoenhut dolls in various positions. The foot is advertising their attributes again. The cover has the more typical advertisement for the "all wood Perfection Art Doll," as well as a notice on packing. The inside of the cover has more pictures and detailed directions for the doll. On the outside base of the box is a label that states, "Character Girl Doll," size 14", curled mohair wig No. 14.

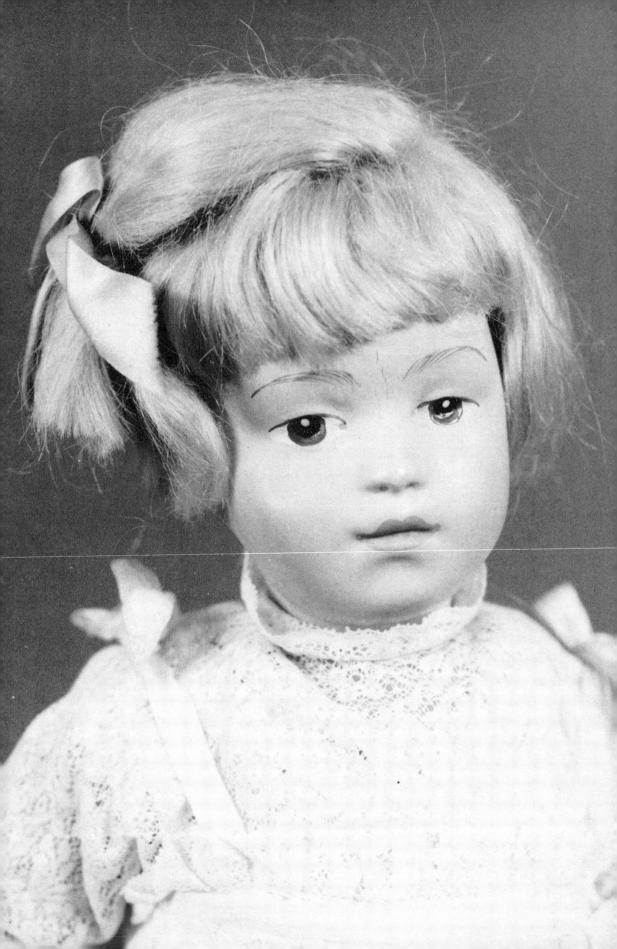

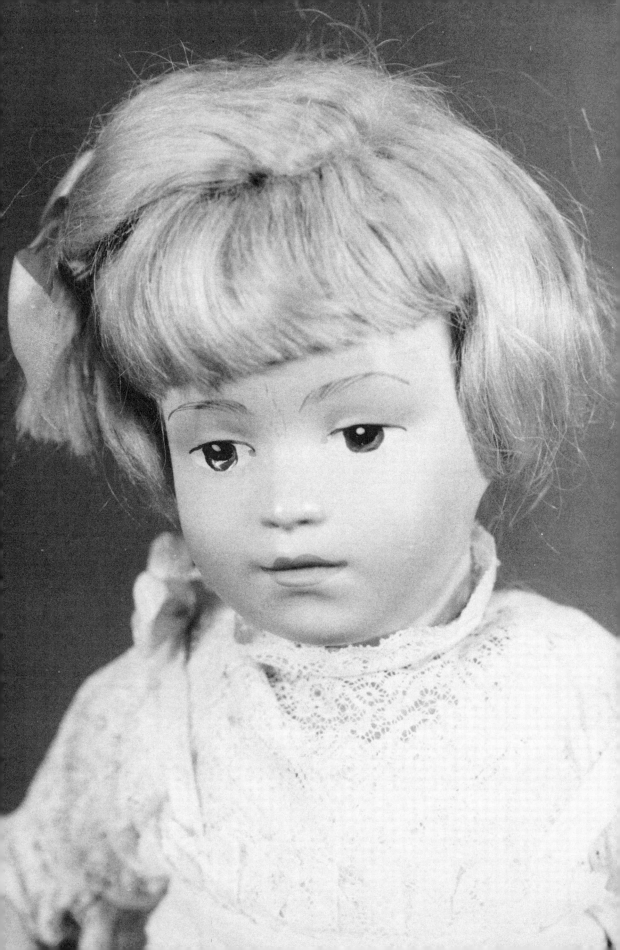

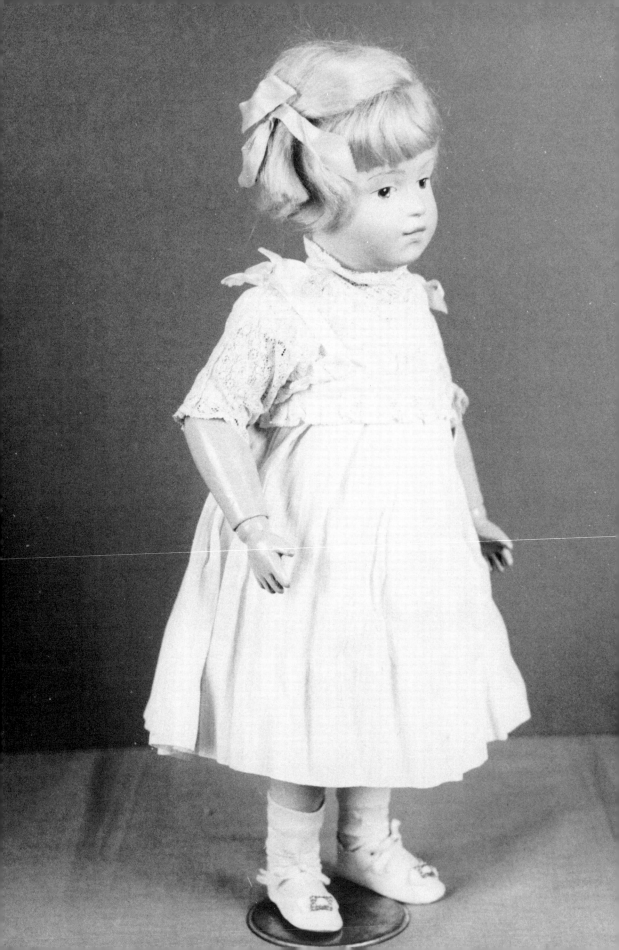

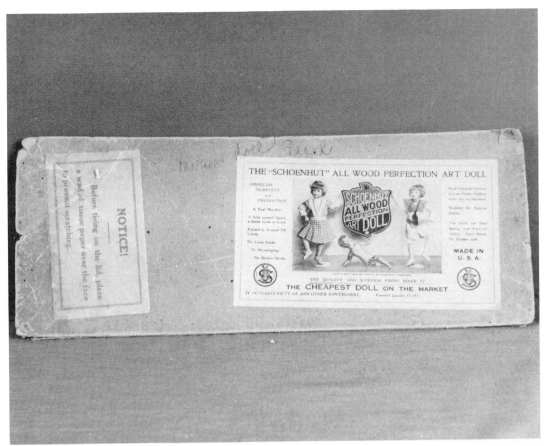

Outside box cover.

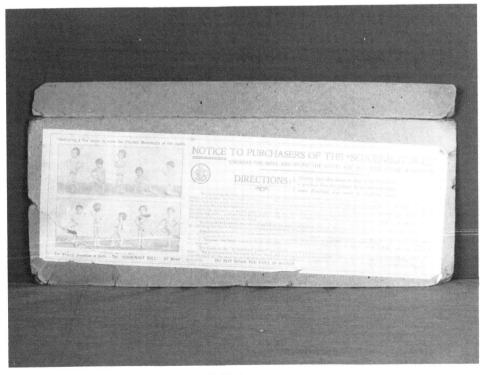

Inside box cover.

Opened box to show how doll is tied in place, then sides fold up.

Sleep-eyed Schoenhut Doll

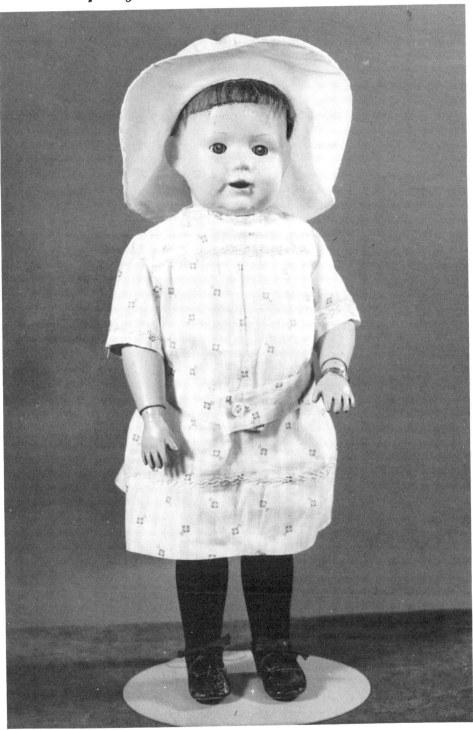

Schoenhut Doll - Seventeen inches high; fully jointed with metal springs, sleeping eyes, open mouth with two inserted metal teeth, wig of human hair. Back incised; Schoenhut Doll/Pat. Jan. 17th, 1911/U.S.A. Mady by A. Schoenhut & Co. of Philadelphia who patented moving eyes for their dolls in 1921. Clothes made in 1921. Bracelet grandmother's wedding band. *Dorothy Lorentzen Collection. Photograph by Richard Merrill.*

Paper Dolls
From the Collection of
the Late Helen Jaques

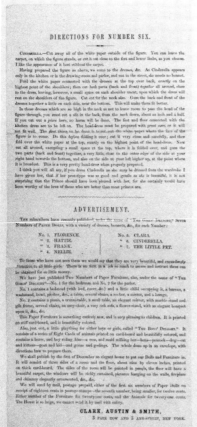

The Girls' Delight is the title of a series of paper dolls by Clark, Austin & Smith, an American manufacturer. The doll pictured is #6, Cinderella, in the series. Although many of the paper dolls were almost identical to those put out by competing companies, the interesting point here is that three of the dresses are nearly identical to a Godey fashion plate from Godey's Lady's Book of 1857. The first photograph shows the original envelope and directions for the paper doll, as well as an advertisement. In the second photograph one can see the Godey fashion plate and the paper doll dresess just below the Godey illustration. *Helen Jaques Collection.*

The May Queen is a paper doll published by Brown, Taggard & Chase, Boston, Massachusetts. The doll is quite large and is intriguing, for in the true sense of the word, she borders on the paper toy or novelty line, as she does not have removable clothes, as one would expect. She is painted in subdued greens and rose. Her hair is deep auburn in color. Her hands are positioned to accept the marvelous garland of flowers. As the May Queen, she wears the crown and veil, with the garland framing her face. As the Shepherdess, she wears the sweet yellow straw hat, carries the crook with its charming bouquet of flowers and also carries the horn, for sheep calling, of course. There is no doubt a May Queen would dress so regally, yet one would never think of a shepherdess in such an ornate, impractical outfit. Obviously, the artist had not ever tended sheep! *Helen Jaques Collection.*

A collage of early handmade paper dolls, framing a small water color of children playing with dolls and a doll house. Each paper doll has the one outfit that is removable. As can be readily seen, the dolls are varied in style and quality of art work. It is an interesting insight into the variety of styles and proportions of the handmade paper doll. *Helen Jaques Collection.*

The Singer Fashion Series

Especially designed by Elizabeth Lesser for making upon Singer Machine N. 66. On the back of each sheet there are suggestions about fabrics and trims. There are directions for making the garments, except the Wedding Gown. Patterns for the outfits were available, except for the Wedding Gown, for ten cents from the Economy Pattern Co., 132 Nasson Street, New York. *Mary Kiley Collection. Photographs by Richard Merrill.*

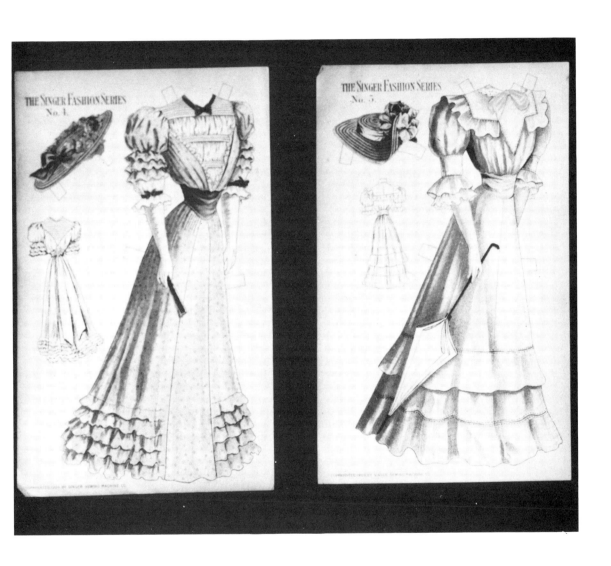

Princess Paper Doll

"OUR PRINCESS"
"To dress with different outfits"
"M & B, Legally Protected, Series 13"
This charming little paper doll comes in a box, measuring 10½" by 5¼" and ¾" deep, which opens on the left, envelope-style. The drawings on the outside and inside cover are done in gold. The coloring of the doll and her costumes is clear and vibrant. Ten inches tall, she appears to be a portrait doll with an appealing smile and inquisitive eyes. *Mary Kiley Collection. Photograph by Richard Merrill.*

M. E. WILMER.
DOLL.

No. 575,749.   Patented Jan. 26, 1897.

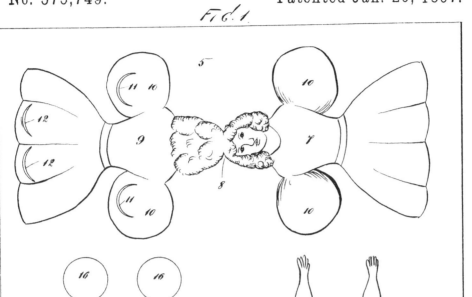

FIG.1

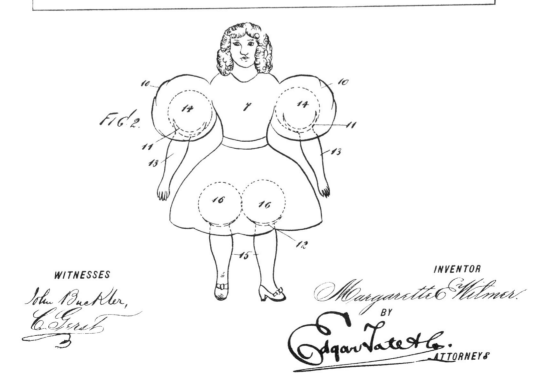

FIG.2

WITNESSES

John Buckler,

C. Gerst

INVENTOR

Margarette Wilmer.

BY

Edgar Tate & Co.

ATTORNEYS

UNITED STATES PATENT OFFICE.

MARGARETTE E. WILMER, OF BROOKLYN, NEW YORK.

DOLL.

SPECIFICATION forming part of Letters Patent No. 575,749, dated January 26, 1897.

Application filed July 9, 1896. Serial No. 598,565. (No model.)

To all whom it may concern:

Be it known that I, MARGARETTE E. WIL-MER, a citizen of the United States, and a resident of Brooklyn, in the county of Kings and
5 State of New York, have invented certain new and useful Improvements in Systems for Making Dolls or Toys, of which the following is a specification, reference being had to the accompanying drawings, forming a part there-
10 of, in which similar numerals of reference indicate corresponding parts wherever found throughout the several views.

This invention relates to the manufacture or construction of dolls and other toy figures,
15 and the object thereof is to provide an improved system for construction or forming dolls or other toy figures from pasteboard, cardboard, or other paper possessing strength and stiffness or from any suitable fabric pos-
20 sessing the required qualities.

The invention is fully disclosed in the following specification, of which the accompanying drawings form a part, and in which—

Figure 1 is a view of a blank from which a
25 toy or doll may be made, and Fig. 2 a face view of a doll made therefrom.

In the practice of my invention I employ a suitable sheet 5, of paper or similar material, and I print, paint, stamp, or otherwise form
30 thereof a face view of a doll, as shown at 7, said view being composed of a head, body, and a portion of the arms, and connected therewith at the top of the head, as shown at 8, is a back view of the same figure, as shown
35 at 9, said back view being also printed, painted, stamped, or otherwise formed, and both of said views may be formed by a suitable stamp at the same time and may be colored as required. Each of these views has a portion
40 of the arms connected therewith, as shown at 10, and the arm portions 10 of the back view are provided with segmental or crescent-shaped marks 11, the convex sides of which are directed downwardly, and in the lower
45 part of the skirt, as shown at 12, are formed similar marks, and I also stamp, print, paint, or otherwise form upon the same sheet the lower portion of the arms, as shown at 13, and the ends thereof, which represent the elbows,
50 are provided with circular heads 14, and stamped, printed, painted, or otherwise formed upon the same sheet are the lower portion of

the legs, as shown at 15, and said legs are provided at that portion thereof which represents the knees with circular heads or disks 16. 55

In forming the doll or toy the figures 7 and 9, which represent the front and back thereof, are cut out in the usual manner, and segmental or crescent-shaped slots are formed at 11 and 12, and the arms 13 and the legs 15 are 60 also cut out, and the circular heads or disks· 14 of the arms are inserted through the slots 11, or that portion of the doll or toy which constitutes the back, and the circular disks or heads 16 of the legs are inserted through the 65 slots 12, and the front and back are then folded together in the usual manner, and a face or front view of a doll thus formed is shown in Fig. 2.

It will be understood that the front and 70 back, after being cut out and folded together as described, may also be sealed or otherwise secured together, and when thus formed it will be apparent that the arms and legs will be free to move laterally or otherwise and 75 that the means by which they are connected with the body portion of the toy or doll when the latter is viewed from the front will be concealed.

It will be apparent that the front and back 80 views may be connected at other parts thereof as well as at the head or instead of at the head, and my invention is not limited to the form of the figure, toy, or doll thus made, as various animals or representations thereof 85 may be similarly formed.

Having fully described my invention, I claim as new and desire to secure by Letters Patent—

1. A doll or toy which is formed by first 90 stamping a front and back view of the figure to be formed on a suitable sheet of paper or similar material in such manner that said front and back views are connected at one point, and may be cut out and folded together 95 so as to form the front and back of the figure, said front and back consisting of a head, body portion, and a portion of the arms, said sheet being also provided with representations of the arms and legs, or the lower portion there- 100 of, said arms and said legs being provided at the ends thereof, which represent the elbows and the knees with circular heads or disks and the back view of said figure being pro-

vided with circular or crescent-shaped marks in that portion of the arms which are formed thereon, and with similar marks in the lower portion of the body or skirt, substantially as shown and described.

2. A doll or toy which is formed by stamping a front and back view of the figure upon a sheet of paper or similar material, said front and back views each comprising the body portion, the head, and the upper portion of the arms, and being connected at the top of the head, said back view being also provided in that portion of the arms connected therewith, with curved or semicircular marks, and at the lower portion of the body with similar marks, said sheet being also provided with representations of the lower portions of the arms and legs, which are provided at the ends which represent the elbows and the knees with circular heads or disks said circular heads or disks being adapted to be inserted when cut out through slots formed at the points where the curved or segmental marks are made in the back portion or view, after said back and front portions have been cut out and folded together, substantially as shown and described.

3. A doll, comprising front and back portions cut from a sheet of paper, and connected at one point, and adapted to be folded together, said front and back portions comprising the body, the head and the upper portion of the arms, the lower portion of the arms and legs being also cut from said sheet of paper, and provided at the ends thereof, which represent the elbows and knees with circular heads or disks which are inserted through slots, substantially as shown and described.

In testimony that I claim the foregoing as my invention I have signed my name, in presence of the subscribing witnesses, this 2d day of July, 1896.

MARGARETTE E. WILMER.

Witnesses:
    W. W. HILL,
    CHARLES S. ROGERS.

Twice Upon a Time

by Betty Thacher

Stories never begin with "twice upon a time," but this story could well begin with that phrase. Twice upon a time, two German doll heads were for sale in Boston, newly imported, not yet antique, and their extraordinary histories since then tell a tale of surprising coincidence.

The first doll caught my eye more than two years ago when our doll club visited the Wenham Museum's magnificent exhibit of dolls and toys. She was a brunette china shoulder-head at the front of a display case, her painted features and hair showing the effects of her experience in the Great Boston Fire of November 9 and 10, 1872. Her history testified to her having been picked out of the ruins of the Heyer Brothers building at 100 Summer Street by Fire Chief John S. Damrell. Elizabeth Donoghue, Curator of Dolls at the Wenham Museum, wrote an article on this doll head entitled "Rescued by the Chief" which was printed in the Regional Souvenir Publication, 1972 Colonial Williamsburg meeting of the Dollology Club of Washington, D.C., U.F.D.C. The article traced the peregrinations of the doll head during the past one hundred years since her rescue from the ruins of Heyer Brothers "importers of fancy goods, toys, musical instruments, baskets, clocks, children's carriages, etc." Most of those things burned, of course, being made of wood, glue and paper. But the large doll head, 7" tall, 5½" wide, was still recognizable and worth retrieving as a souvenir. Chief Damrell gave the head to Mrs. Joseph Barnes. In 1898, it passed from her to Elizabeth Richards Horton, owner of one of the biggest doll collections in America. How early this hobby is! Mrs. Horton's collection included the famous Columbia, who travelled around the world. In 1922, Mrs. Horton gave her collection to the Wenham Museum in Wenham, Massachusetts, and ever since the German fraulein has surveyed passersby and collectors with her blue eyes, faded by her experience in the dreadful Boston Fire.

This terrifying two-day fire devastated seventy acres around Washington and Summer Streets, Boston's business center. Eight hundred buildings were demolished, more than one thousand businesses were affected, and property damaged in the amount of over 100 million dollars, according to statistics in Mrs. Donoghue's article. In one record book, Heyer Brothers is listed as having lost a $100,000 business. One of the twelve people who died as a result of the fire was a member of the firm of Heyer Brothers who returned to the building to retrieve records and was fatally injured when a wall crumbled and fell on him. He was my great grandfather. His wife was Caroline Heyer.

The name Heyer Brothers leaped out of the Wenham Museum showcase at me because I had heard the story of the Boston Fire many times from my mother, along with descriptions of the fine German toys her grandfather's family had imported for many years. Yet no one in the family had any of these delightful things remaining. The faded head in the Wenham Museum was the only one any one in the family had ever seen. I pointed it out to the other members of the doll club, and later told my mother, who was as fascinated as I was at this haunting relic of the past. So interested was Mother, that she researched family information on the Heyer Brothers company and sent it to the Museum for their records, and Mrs. Donoghue in turn sent her copies of the changes in ownership of the doll head, and a reprint of her article on the Boston Fire and the doll business. For example, two hundred girls who were employed sixteen weeks a year in doll dressing, were thrown out of work by the fire. A number of others made toys and they also lost their jobs. What an impact on the local economy this must have had - - and less than eight weeks before Christmas.

Naturally I wished I had a family souvenir from the Heyer Brothers stock. What could be nicer for a doll collector today than a family doll from long ago. But there were none.

Then twice upon a time did happen. At the June meeting of our doll club, a friend came with a tissue-wrapped package which she gave me with, "Betty, you should have this; it came from Heyer Brothers."

It was astonishing, but it surely did come from Heyer Brothers after 108 years. It was the head of a second German fraulein, a placid looking, blue eyed girl with a double chin, blond molded hair with a flat center part, curls at the temples and ears, and a white bisque complexion. She has brown eyebrows with pink cheeks and mouth that the heat of the fire turned beige-brown. She is similar in size to the first head pulled from the ashes in 1872, measuring 6" high and 5½" wide.

Unmistakably marked inside the head in an old-fashioned hand, pencilled over the soot staining the bisque, is the record "Boston Fire Nov. 9 & 10 '72 Hyer Bros W" trailing off into the indecipherable. Stuffed inside the doll's head were two papers corroborating her genealogy. One is a newspaper clipping dated Feb. 1963 from the Lynn, MA, *Daily Item*, picturing Miss Olive J. Benedict. The other is a handwritten dab of information on part of a Christmas card and dated June, 1963, stating the "Doll belonged to Olive Benedict, given to me by Elinor Stark, her friend, June 1963." The card is unsigned. It is possible the doll may have been in the collection of a Lexington, MA, woman named Beckwith, and perhaps she

is the unknown "me." Also handwritten on the card is a brief account of how the Boston Fire was believed to have begun in the establishment of Messrs. Tibbitts, Baldwin & Davis, wholesale dry goods dealers.

My generous friend who gave me the doll head from her own collection has told me as much as she knows about it. Perhaps there are other collectors who knew Olive J. Benedict or Elinor Stark and who could furnish information on their interests. Perhaps they were not collectors of dolls, but were local historians. Wherever this doll head travelled, it is an amazing coincidence that of all the many souvenirs that surely were picked up in 1872 in the fire ruins (granted the proclivity of the human race for souvenir hunting), two should be doll heads, and one should have come to me, a descendant who coincidentally happens to like antique dolls.

Author's doll head from Heyer Bros. that survived the 1872 Boston Fire.

Doll head from 1872 Boston Fire on exhibit at the Wenham Museum.

Recollections of Tynietoy Doll Houses And Doll House Furniture

by Herbert H. Hosmer

Curator, The Toy Cupboard Museum, South Lancaster, Massachusetts

Photography by Joseph Kurklen

Many miniature collectors, as well as doll and toy collectors, who recall the years between World War I and World War II will remember Tynietoy Doll Houses and Doll House Furniture and Accessories. Tynietoy is not to be confused with the popular Tootsietoy metal miniatures which were a small scale. Tynietoy was constructed of wood and was one inch to the foot in scale. The Tynietoy production was one of the earliest attempts to create a line of skillfully hand-crafted dolls' houses and doll house furniture, copied after American antiques in the best known period designs. By today's standards the prices seem very modest indeed but in the scale of values of the time the prices seemed higher than average miniatures then on sale.

Miss Marion I. Perkins and her associate Miss Amy Vernon were the two ladies from Providence, Rhode Island who established this unique enterprise which flourished just a little more than twenty years, roughly 1920 to 1943. Another World War brought an end to this intriguing and artistic endeavor and now some forty years later dolls' houses and doll house furniture marked with the Tynietoy trade-mark are much sought after by a legion of miniature collectors.

Miss Perkins was an interior decorator who had a skill in making miniature copies of antique furniture and Miss Vernon was deeply concerned in developing social services for disabled veterans from World War I and for elderly or retired or artistic people who had no way to market their creativity.

Starting modestly, one of the first acknowledgments of the combined endeavor of these two ladies, was an article entitled "A Doll's House That Could Not Fail To Make A Merry Christmas" in the issue of The Ladies' Home Journal for November 1920. No author is listed for this article and no mention is made of Miss Perkins or Miss Vernon by name, other than to say that "Two women were the builders, assisted by a convalescent soldier, and what two women have done, one woman can do (with or without the aid of a man) by taking a little longer time." But there is no question of the origin of this house or it's furnishings. A floor plan with measurements is shown as well as an interior and an exterior photograph of the house as completed. In future catalogues, put out almost annually, by Tynietoy this house is shown under the title of The Nantucket House.

Although almost identical in every detail, the house in the catalogues was enlarged by one more room, the addition of a kitchen lean-to ell. In the house described and shown in The Ladies' Home Journal, the salt box house had only a parlor and combined kitchen and dining area on the ground floor with a bedroom and attic or bathroom area under the sweep of the salt box roof. The addition to the house, as advertised in the catalogues, had the added ell so had the advantage of parlor, dining room and kitchen on the ground floor. The photograph of the interior, in the article, shows the rooms furnished with such familiar Tynietoy furniture as the four-poster canopy bed, the Sheraton sofa, the round Sheraton table, the 18th century card table (viewed through the parlor archway to the small front hall) and in the kitchen-dining room the dresser for dishes and the wooden sink with drain board. The exterior photograph of the finished house shows the ladder-back, rush-seated settee, which came later in black or Chinese red, lined and decorated, or in natural stain. The extended Nantucket House in later catalogues had hollyhocks painted here and there against the outside walls as well as a picket fence and dooryard garden. In 1920, as well as in all later designs, the Nantucket House included a "Widow's Walk" on the ridgepole of the house and this was reached by a ladder from inside the second floor bedroom.

Advertising in national magazines such as House Beautiful and others, soon brought prestigeous patronage and the staff of crafts-people was augmented by artistic men and women who were involved in construction, finishing and painting at the shop or at home. A full-time staff of approximately fourteen was more or less usual at the shop, but many part-time artists assisted too, including the

The New England Town House by Tynietoy, Providence, R.I. In the 1920s and '30s this sold for $85.00 unfurnished. By the late '30s it was $98.00 unfurnished!

Colonial Kitchen in pine - One inch to the foot. Vertical sheathing. All furniture is from same designs as Tynietoy. By George Le Clerc.

Panelled Room with inlaid floor - One inch to the foot. All furniture is from same designs as Tynietoy and the upholstery is real fabric. By George Le Clerc.

Victorian Parlor. Pedestal base table with top painted to represent marble - Black walnut sofa and arm chair - upholstery painted black to represent horsehair. Soft metal fruit dish to represent silver - with fruit. Woven rug.

The Painted Bedroom - Typical of country homes in the 1920s.

Large scale Sheraton type chairs - mahogany stain - two different designs. Upholstered seats in real fabric. These chairs are by George Le Clerc.

Tea Table - 18th century - in natural wood - signed George Le Clerc. Chippendale Chair in natural wood with upholstered seat in real fabric. These are the large scale pieces by George Le Clerc.

Wing Chair painted to represent chintz and with stained mahogany feet. Maple Low-boy with wooden knobs and shell decoration painted to represent carving on center drawer. Coffee set - coffee pot, creamer, cup and saucer and spoon, on tray. Soft metal to suggest silver - from Tynietoy Accessories List.

students of the Rhode Island School of Design who were frequently called upon. For many years upholstery was simulated by painted designs to represent chintz and brocade but some later pieces were actually upholstered in miniscule patterned fabrics of silk or soft velvet.

A line of accessories - - tableware, household utensils, garden equipment - - were imported from Germany and other sources but hand-woven rugs were a very special item, loom-woven in miniature in Providence. One could order old-time window shades or curtains and urn-shaped table lamps of turned wood came complete with hand-painted and decorated parchment shades. Similar floor lamps were also available.

In a late catalogue, circa 1940, a list of stores and toy shops in major cities across the United States where Tynietoy dolls' houses and doll house furniture were available, takes up the whole inside cover and gives some idea of the popularity of these miniatures from coast to coast.

George Henry Le Clerc (1894-1972), who became chief production manager under Miss Perkins and Miss Vernon, was a master craftsman and miniature maker. After he left Tynietoy to pursue his own career, he made beautifully paneled and inlaid rooms both at one inch to the foot and in a larger scale. The smaller rooms are furnished with the same pieces of furniture that he made for Tynietoy at one inch to the foot. The chairs and sofas in these rooms are upholstered in real silks and velvets and brocades and the curtains that match are all said to have been the work of Mrs. Le Clerc. The large scale rooms are furnished with fine and detailed examples of identified pieces of antique furniture after Chippendale, Sheraton and Hepplewhite. Occasionally pieces are signed with his name and in one instance, a maple Empire sideboard, the piece is both signed George Le Clerc and stamped Tynietoy. Tynietoy used paper labels and a stamp pressed or burned into the wood. Some pieces can only be identified from the illustrated catalogues since there was no surface big enough to take the paper label or the stamp but there is a style of design that identifies Tynietoy furniture and the advanced collector recognizes this quality almost instinctively.

The Tynietoy Preservation Society at the Toy Cupboard Museum in South Lancaster, Massachusetts, includes the Tynietoy collection of the Director and extensive examples of Tynietoy furniture and accessories and of the Le Clerc rooms and furniture in both scales. All these are on view including the largest Tynietoy dolls' house, The Colonial Mansion, bought by the author in 1933 and furnished during the years 1928 to 1933.

Tynietoy trademark stamped or pressed into the under side of the Maple Low-boy with wooden knobs. This late trademark is the familiar one but bears the legend - Tynietoy Inc. Prov. RI. T.M. REG.

Also in the Tynietoy area is The New England Town House, bought at an auction in 1978 and a replica of the Nantucket House made exactly from the plan in the November 1920 issue of *The Ladies' Home Journal*. This replica is the work of Mr. Milville Davey and his wife Elizabeth, of Wakefield, Rhode Island. The Daveys worked for Tynietoy from the 1920s up to about 1935. They met at Tynietoy and have been married ever since. Mr. Davey now restores and reproduces Tynietoy furniture but carefully stamps the pieces with his name and the present date. Mrs. Davey recently presented the Tynietoy Preservation Society with a certificate of stock in Tynietoy, presented to her on February 14, 1928. All Tynietoy employees were presented stock in the company, I understand. Mrs. Davey's certificate is No. 84. Mrs. Davey painted the hollyhocks on the Nantucket House just as she did nearly sixty years ago. She has painted all the upholstered pieces, wing chair and chair seats for the furniture Mr. Davey has reproduced exactly like the old pieces.

Mr. Herbert Durling who worked for over a year at Tynietoy, as a young man literally just out of high school, attends the annual meetings of the Tynietoy Preservation Society. He was at Tynietoy just as the company was phasing out around 1942. His recollections of those final months compliment the recollections of Mr. and Mrs. Davey in the period of 1920 and 1930.

Identifying Door of Hope Dolls

by Mary Eveline Sicard

Photography by Richard Merrill

It has long been a popular practice for foreign missionaries around the world to encourage native craftsmen to create dolls that depicted representative members of their respective societies. From Asia, in the wake of intense missionary effort in the latter half of the nineteenth century and first half of the twentieth century, have come an abundance of these mission-made dolls, historically interesting in their handmade native garments. From the diverse provinces of China came a medley of dolls; from Canton, from Peking, and P'ao Ting Fu. Unquestionably, the dolls from the Door of Hope Mission in Shanghai stand apart from other mission-sponsored dolls in the exceptional excellence of their handworked carving and costumes, and in the large number of characters illustrating such a broad panorama of social levels and occupations.

Because there were so many different dolls created, confusion sometimes arises in Door of Hope doll identification. After a brief résumé of the mission's history, illustrations of the dolls are presented here with the hope that some of the confusion may be diminished.

The Mission

Shanghai. 1901. In this teeming seaport, largest of all cities in China, a small group of caring foreign women formed an alliance called the Committee for Chinese Rescue Work, to help alleviate the sufferings of young Chinese females who had been sold into slavery or prostitution. On November 21, 1901, they opened a sanctuary, a supportive haven where abused children and girls could be lovingly rehabilitated in an atmosphere of acceptance and Christian guidance. They called this home, the Door of Hope. "Our door is plain and unpretentious, but it has been God's Door of Hope to thousands of poor girls and children." These were the words of Cornelia Leavenworth Bonnell who first administered the operation, and she continued poignantly, "In the Home where I live and which is located in the district where all the houses of sin are, we take in at any hour of day or night girls and children who run away to us themselves or are sent in by the police. They go on to our permanent Homes or wherever each case needs to be sent. So we have an always changing family and it is Mrs. Woo's duty to look after them while they are here and give them as much as possible of the gospel which is the power of God unto salvation."[1]

The determined efforts of the dedicated committee members and staff succeeded so effectively that before many years had passed a network of operations had been established. In 1908 there were five separate Homes operating under the umbrella of the Door of Hope. They were the Receiving Home where new arrivals (predominantly from the Shanghai Municipal Court) were evaluated; two First Year Homes called the Love School and the New Heart School; the Industrial Home where the older girls lived who still wished to remain with the mission after they had completed their first year's rehabilitative term and a Children's Home located five miles from Shanghai in the countryside of Chiangwan.

Financial support for the mission was derived from varied sources. Some contributions were dependable and regular such as the grant from the Shanghai Municipal Council earmarked for the support of the Receiving Home and the funds from the Christian Herald in America for the operation of the Children's Home. Other supplementary revenue came from legacies, memorials, private donations of service groups and individuals both Chinese and foreign, and the sponsorship from the homelands of assigned "love-daughters." The need for funds was persistent as the operations expanded and the sale of embroidered handcrafts from the Industrial Home and the sale of dolls from the First Year Homes helped significantly to ease the increasing financial requirements.

Through the ensuing years, ever-present, was a devoted evangelism and an optimistic faith in God's intent to protect them in the face of precarious social and political upheaval. In 1939, the Japanese occupation of Shanghai was in full force. Mission activities were carried on sporadically until the hiatus through World War Two. Finally, in 1950, the establishment of Communist government resulted in the abandonment of the mission in Shanghai. Under the directorship of long-time staffer E. Gladys Dieterle, the Door of Hope was re-established in 1953 in Taiwan, but it was operated as a girls' home with the emphasis on

EXQUISITE CHINESE DOLLS

❖❖❖

AS RED is the Chinese color of hope and new life, this little bride wears brightest scarlet satin, stiff with elaborate tucks and embroideries. The handsome groom is similarly decked in satin but of a richer, more sober hue, while high boots and hat with a long, slender quill adds to his elegance. These dolls must be seen to appreciate the delicate carving of their wooden faces and the exquisite needlework of their clothes. They are the ultimate in dolls!

Finest Hand-Made Chinese Dolls.

D410—Chinese Bride, 11"........$9.95
D411—Chinese Groom, 11".......9.95

IN troubled Shanghai are made the finest Chinese dolls, by reclaimed girls working in a mission-haven. Some of them carve from smooth, creamy wood the Oriental faces and delicate hands; others lightly tint the serene countenances into a tiny, life-like flush. Then miniature garments and under-garments of finest silk and linen are made with exacting care, each complete with bindings, linings and minute fastenings. You will delight in their perfection and have an increasing pride in possessing these treasures.

CHANG THE CHINESE FARMER

CARVED from wood like ivory by a master Chinese craftsman are the gentle impassive features of Chang the Farmer. From under the broad brim of his woven coolie hat, he will look at sorrow, crop failure, and famine with the same fatalistic calm with which he greets prosperity. His broad shoulders are bowed as much by the weight of care as by the weight of the queer straw raincoat. Chang wears the garments of coarse blue cloth which is typical of his class and is barefoot. You will not find a more unusual figure.

Hand Carved and Hand Dressed In China

No. D409—Chang, 12 inches high $6.50

Sp. on Bridal Pr.	$18.00
Old Lady	6.25
Old Gentleman	6.25
Young Lady, 10"	6.25
Young Gentleman	6.25
Boy in Silk, 8"	4.95

Girl in Silk, 7"	$4.95
Small Boy, 6½"	4.45
Small Girl, 6½"	4.45
Amah and Baby	7.50
Table Boy	4.95
Priest	4.95

Mourner	$4.95
Widow	4.95
Policeman	6.50
Manchu Woman	6.95
Amah	4.95

Most Dolls above are 11"

THIS MARVELOUS GROUP OF EIGHTEEN DOLLS COSTS OVER $109.00, SPECIAL FOR GROUP $95.00

OLD MAN　　　PRIEST　　　AMAH　　　MOURNER

Illustration 1. Kimport Sales Sheet.

education, and domestic pursuits and crafts were no longer in the foreground of daily occupations.

The Dolls

The dolls were assembled and dressed by the girls in the First Year Homes assisted by Chinese helpers on the staff. This description, from mission reports, allows us a glimpse at the procedure: "Many who come to us have never taken any care of themselves, never used a needle, and can neither read nor write. Their mornings in this Home, therefore, are given up to study while in the afternoon they are taught to sew. They first learn to make all their own clothing and when they can do this, they are allowed to do the finer work of making and dressing Chinese model dolls, the sale of which is a substantial help toward the upkeep of this Home."

According to mission records, production of the dolls began in 1902. Twenty-four characters were illustrated in a photo and their identities listed in the annual report for 1940. They were called the "Door of Hope Model Dolls" and represented:

1. Bride
2. Bridegroom
3. Old Lady
4. Old Gentleman
5. Young Lady
6. Young Lady in Long Garment
7. Young Gentleman
8. Boy in Silk
9. Girl in Silk
10. Small Boy in Silk
11. Small Girl in Silk
12. School Girl (in Cotton)
13. School Boy (in Cotton)
14. Kindergarten Child
15. Baby
16. Cantonese Amah and Baby
17. Amah
18. Table Boy
19. Priest
20. Mourner
21. Widow
22. Policeman
23. Farmer
24. Manchu Woman

Dolls that portrayed characters from other social roles and occupations were occasionally made also, though they are scarce and can be considered important additions to the basic set. (See Nurse and Nun in Illustration 12.)

The dolls were sold directly on order from the mission and through a mission crafts store in Shanghai. They were distributed in the USA by Kimport and Elsie Clark Krug as well as retail import stores like Yamanaka's in New

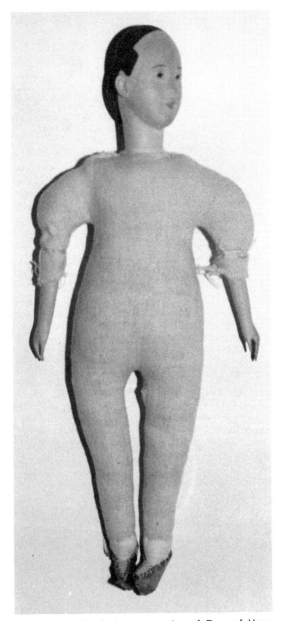

Illustration 2. Body construction of Door of Hope doll.

York. Furloughed missionaries used them on their return to their homelands to illustrate the lives of Chinese people in fundraising programs.

When Kimport introduced their *Doll Talk Magazine* in 1936, a full page separate sales sheet devoted exclusively to the Door of Hope Dolls was included (see illustration 1). Nineteen dolls were offered at a special price of $95.00. The bride and groom were priced at $18.00 for the pair. Individual prices ranged from $9.95 for the bride alone, to $4.45 for the small boy or girl in silk; all substantial prices for the times.

149

The turbulent war-ravaged years between 1939 and 1947 include a gap in the normal scope of mission accomplishments. In the Spring of 1943 Kimport's then well-established *Doll Talk* was almost entirely given over to the subject of the Dolls of China, but the recap of the Door of Hope Mission stated that "supplies are extinct." For information purposes, a list of the dolls that had been available was printed which included the addition of a twenty-fifth character, a "Modern Bride." There are two variant brides which differ from the traditional early Bride with her elaborate large round Manchurian beaded and pom-pommed headdress and tiny shoes for bound feet. These alternate brides may well be called "Modern Brides" since they both exhibit the flat-soled shoes for unbound feet, a mark of modernism after the establishment of the Republic in 1911. Their bridal clothes are nearly identical to the embroidered red satin garments of the traditional bride, but each of their headdresses vary from hers; are not as elaborate and lack a veil.

After World War Two ended, Arthur McKim of Kimport wrote to the Door of Hope to inquire about purchasing dolls once again. In August, 1947, he received a reply informing him that the mission's "internment" was over and that dolls were once again available, but careful review of the editions of *Doll Talk* from then through 1950 show not a single mention of Door of Hope dolls for sale though other types of native handcrafted dolls from China are featured.

In the nineteen-thirties also, a small number of Door of Hope dolls had been distributed by Elsie Clark Krug, a well-known collector/dealer from Baltimore who communicated with her customers by means of a chatty informative monthly newsletter. Her January/February 1958 newsletter described the Door of Hope Mission and the doll-making project as well as a chronicle of her vain attempts to acquire dolls from the mission after 1939. In a recent letter to her old friend and customer, Ruth Whittier, Elsie explained her early distribution of Door of Hope dolls: "In 1932 when I was in Shanghai, I visited the Door of Hope . . . When I went to the Door of Hope I was at the start of a trip around the world. . . . I took what dolls were on hand at the time and ordered more to follow. But already there was political unrest in Shanghai and my order was never filled." In her April 1943 newsletter, Elsie listed a lone Priest, a remnant surely, reiterating that no Door of Hope dolls had arrived since the Japanese occupation of Shanghai.

Construction of the Dolls

The marvelous countenances of the dolls command instant interest. Carved in a wood that echoes the color of oriental complexion, and with simply but deftly painted hair arrangements, the dolls' heads approach near-perfect life modelling.

In Elsie Krug's 1958 description, the wood is reported to be Chinese Pear wood, but new data now reveal that the wood used for the heads is the genus Euonymus. After analyzing slivers of wood removed from two different dolls, Miss Donna Cristensen of the Center for Wood Anatomy Research, at the United States Forest Products Laboratory, issued a report to the author stating, in part, "Confirming our telephone conversation, the wood samples from both dolls have been identified as *Euonymus*. The exact species cannot be determined since we have nothing in our files on those native to China." Included in the report was a technical description of Euonymus with the information that the majority of the more than 175 species of Euonymus occurs mostly from the Himalaya Mountains to China and Japan. Of the few species native to North America, we are most familiar with the Burning Bush, Spindle Tree and Bittersweet. The gross characteristics of Euonymus parallel those of fruit trees in general in the color of the bark and wood as well as density.

The bodies of the Door of Hope dolls were simply designed and constructed of two main pieces, front and back, of rough unbleached cotton handseamed along the perimeter and stuffed with cotton batting. (see illus. 2) The lower parts of the legs, starting just above the ankle and descending and tapering to what would be the bottom of the heel, were covered with a sewn-on smooth white cotton which simulated socks. (Two exceptions in the basic group are the Farmer and the Manchu Woman whose lower legs are of carved wood.) The fronts of the feet were formed by stuffing the shoe with cotton batting and covering the mound with sewn-down scraps of the same white cloth used in the "socks." The stuffed shoe was sewn to the body at the ankles.

The bottoms of the wooden necks and the tops of the wooden arms have channels carved around them to enable them to be tied into the neck and arm openings of the cloth bodies. After the heads and limbs have been set into place, the cloth of the body openings was drawn up and over the channel and strong cotton thread was wound several times around and stitched down. Occasionally, wooden arms were NOT used in the completion of a

Illustration 3. *Left to right:* Traditional Bride 11½'';
Bridegroom 12¼''. They wear the most colorful and
strikingly embroidered garments; the bride in bright
red, and the groom in a deep plum. The bridal veil is
worn in front of the face, not to be removed until the
bride enters the nuptual room at the groom's house.
Occasionally, the Bridegroom is found wearing a
white, straw-like conical hat with red silk tassel
radiating from the center and with a globular rank
button at the apex. This hat is a civil official's summer
hat, similar to that worn by the Policeman (see
Illustration 12) but subtly more ornate.

Illustration 4. Traditional Bride and Young Lady.
Here is the Bride without her headdress. Note the
carved and colored flowerbuds decorating her hair.
All three Brides have flowers of varying arrangements in their hair. In China, as elsewhere, women
signified their married status by drawing their hair
back up into a bun. In some parts of China it was the
custom also to pluck the front forehead hair the night
before the marriage or on the wedding day before the
bride left home. With the assistance of close female
relatives or friends, the plucking was executed by
rolling the clipped forehead hair between two tautly
held threads.

Illustration 5. Modern Girl Bride 11½″. The immediate difference between this lovely Bride and the traditional bride is the change of hats. Notice that this Bride's hat does not have a veil and that she has flat-soled shoes indicating unbound feet. *Madeline Merrill Collection.*

Illustration 6. Old Gentleman 12"; Old Lady 11"; Young Gentleman 12"; Young Lady 11½". The quality of the fine silks and silk-satins used in dressing these four dolls gives instant recognition of their high social status. The somber colors connote dignity. The Old Gentleman wears soft gray and plum and the Old Lady wears a deep plum jacket and black silk skirt. In addition to the carved facial wrinkles and hollowed cheeks, their hair has been deftly painted to illustrate aging. The Young Gentleman, in pastel blue and gray, wears blue silk leggings under his robe.. The Young Lady's jacket displays decorative costume accents such as the double collar and fluted closure. She wears a lavishly beaded cap and she wears tiny sharply pointed shoes to signify bound feet as does the Old Lady and the Traditional Bride.

doll's body and it was left with arms only in stubs. This practice was not consistent with any specific character. It occurs at random. A reasonable explanation based on review of mission methods, indicates that the arms were omitted merely because they were not available at the time that particular doll was being assembled. There was no social significance attached to the absence of arms.

Other than size to distinguish age differences, there was no variation in the cloth bodies so the characterization of individuals was achieved in the carving and painting of the heads and in the remarkably duplicated costumes of pre-revolutionary China.

Presented here is a gallery of twenty-six Door of Hope dolls. Twenty-four of them match those on the published lists, almost a full set. Absent from the photos is the Young Lady in Long Garment. She would be recognizable by her long-sleeved full length robe with side closure and mandarin collar, similar to the Manchu Woman (see illus. 11) but without the elaborately carved headdress. All other women in the basic set wear trousers, or skirts over trousers. Also shown here are two rare dolls, the Hospital Nurse and the Buddhist

Girl Nun (see illus. 12). They came as part of a group of twenty-one Door of Hope dolls that had been ordered directly from the mission in 1910 by Miss Edith Weld of Boston and Wareham, Massachusetts, after a talk she'd attended given by Episcopal Suffragen Bishop Theodore Ludlow. Handwritten paper name tags were sewn on to their clothing and in some cases delineate the characterization more clearly than the lists. Specific instances are the already-mentioned Buddhist Girl Nun and Hospital Nurse as well as Farmer IN RAINY DAY CLOTHES; SON IN MOURNING; Widow ON THE DAY OF THE FUNERAL; BUDDHIST MONK; SHANGHAI MUNICIPAL Policeman; and SMALL CHILD for Kindergarten Child, and HOUSE SERVANT for Table Boy.

Attempts to identify Door of Hope dolls that vary from the photos or descriptions given here may be aided by consideration of the following data:

Colors vary in garments of two dolls who appear to be the same character because the mission made the dolls over such a long span of years.

Illustration 7. Baby 6½"; Amah 11½"; Cantonese Amah 11" and Baby 5½"; Kindergarten Child 7". Although all three babies appear to be alike, they differ in size and other details. All three wear bibs and cat caps. Underneath, Baby (in bunting) and Baby with Amah wear a folded strip of cloth extending from waist down through the legs, and up to back waist. It is the Chinese diaper. The older Kindergarten Child, now walking in cat-faced shoes that the others do not wear, no longer needs it. All three wear the traditional split and lapped pants that facilitates toilet training.

Almost all clothing was removable, so loss of hats and exchange of garments occurred.

Garments should fit well if they are on the correct doll.

Trousers, robes and jackets were constructed alike and worn by both sexes, adults and children. Their differences lie in the selection of material and choice of color, both very important to the Chinese of the Ch'ing Dynasty.

Western influence in matters of dress, begun by missionaries and traders in the nineteenth century and intensified by the cultural exchange of World War I propogated a confused blend of East and West. In 1911 the new law of the Republic of China banned the wearing of the queue and the binding of feet. In cosmopolitan Shanghai, though there were many who attempted to adhere to the old customs, the thrust was toward adaptation of modern modes. Some male Door of Hope dolls then, for example the Young Gentleman, will be found with either the traditional queue or with hair painted in a standard western men's style. Even the splendid Bridegroom,

in his elaborate Manchurian robes, will be sometimes be found with a painted western haircut!

Because of the unique direction of the modern history of China under the rise of Communism with the emphasis on isolationism and suppression of those facets of culture which acted as reminders of imperialism, the Door of Hope dolls have achieved an unexpected prominence. Because, in their manufacture, they were faithful mirrors of the people of the times, they present to us today vehicles of instruction into a microcosm of Chinese history that has vanished. They provide our western world with realistic insight into Chinese culture at all levels of society, a most significant contribution since so few museums became the repository for garments and artifacts of common, everyday usage. Winsome and serene and intriguing, they broaden our scope of understanding of China at the same time that they enhance our collections with such excellent examples of doll-making artistry. To all those who participated in their creation and distribution so long ago, we owe our thanks.

Illustration 9. Boy in silk 9''; Small Girl in silk 6¾''. They are not dressed in the heavy silk-satin of the larger pair but in a lighter weight brocade. This little girl's hair is carved in a Dutch Clip and is decorated with a carved bow painted yellow and blue. *Eleanor Harriman Collection.*

Illustration 8. Girl in silk 8¼''; Boy in silk 8¾''; Table Boy 12''; School Girl in cotton 9''; School Boy in cotton 8¾''. The cut of the garments worn by the children in silk and the children in cotton is the same. The fabrics differ, obviously. The Girl in silk appears with a hat utilizing false hair, a popular practice in China. This hat is worn over a painted hairdo of braids which end at the nape of the neck at which point a braid of real hair is added. The Table Boy wears plain blue cotton robe, a p'ao, under a short black jacket with front closure.

Illustration 10. Farmer 12½''; Mourner 12''; Widow 12''. These three dolls are notable for the execution of detail which defines their characterization. The Farmer's carved feet are bare and he wears rolled-up trousers of coarse blue cotton and rolled-up sleeves on his jacket of the same material. His queue has been carved wound around his head, out of his way as he labors. The mourning son and widow wear the hempen robes of close relatives over their white mourning clothes. The widow's hair bar is appropriately painted in silver instead of the more usual gold.

Illustration 11. Manchu Woman. There can be no mistaking the Manchu Woman. She wears a carved headdress, a long robe, and her lower limbs are carved complete with a pedestal, or stilt shoe, of northern China. *Joyce Sefton Collection.*

Illustration 11A: Close-up
of Manchu Woman.

Illustration 12. Priest 12''; Hospital Nurse 11½''; Buddhist Girl Nun 8¼''; Policeman 12¼''. The Priest, shown, has Buddhist scars indented into his scalp. He wears padded clothing, a soft saffron colored robe over dark blue jacket and light blue trousers. His dark blue jacket and round-toed yellow shoes match identically those on the Girl Nun. Her head, however, has not been totally shaved. She has a circlet of fringed hair painted on round a bald pate. The Hospital Nurse wears a starched white apron over a gray and white striped jacket and trousers. Note the insignia worn on her left breast. It is the same as that worn on the left breast of the Policeman. Her hair is carved in a widow's peak and a long braid which is wound around her head. The Policeman wears dark blue wool jacket and pants and black boots. His white hat, with red tassel fringe, is identified by the small gilt button in front and on the top.